PARENTHESES

An Autobiographical Journey

By the Author

JAY NEUGEBOREN

PARENTHESES

*An Autobiographical
Journey*

E. P. DUTTON & CO., INC. NEW YORK 1970

First Edition

Copyright © 1970 by Jay Neugeboren
All rights reserved. Printed in the U.S.A.

Published simultaneously in Canada by
Clarke, Irwin & Company Limited, Toronto and Vancouver

Library of Congress Catalog Card Number: 73-95489

Part of Chapter One appeared in different form in
New American Review No. 5.

A24302   [04]

For Miriam Nancy
and to the memory of
Nancy Cusack

Contents

It must interest us that he [Martin Luther] urged the postponement of monastic vows until the age of thirty—the age when sexual drive has passed its peak, when identity is firmly established, and when man's ideological pliability comes to an end.

—Erik H. Erikson. *Young Man Luther.*

PARENTHESES

An Autobiographical Journey

ONE: *Reflections at Thirty*

The point is that it is almost impossible (except in the form of fiction) to write *in* America *about* America *for* Americans. You can, as an American, go to the South Sea Islands and write upon your return; you can, as a foreigner, travel in America and write upon taking leave; you can, as an immigrant, write as you get settled; you can move from one section of this country or from one "class" of this country to another, and write while you still have one foot in each place. But in the end you always write about the way it feels to arrive or to leave, to change or to get settled. You write about a process of which you are a more or less willing, but always pleasurably harassed, part, and your style soon runs away with you in the high gear of dithyrambic or outraged expression.

—Erik H. Erikson. *Childhood and Society.*

Memorial Day. May 30, 1968. My thirtieth birthday. Up late last night hunting snails by flashlight with Jeannot, a friend. He is gypsy, Spanish. "Domesticated gypsy," Betsey and I say. Jeannot has three children, works with his wife Jacqueline doing silk-screen designs. It has been raining these last few days, our tub of snails grows. More humid than usual. I spend my time writing, gardening, and listening to the radio for news of the revolution in France. The entire country shut down for thirteen days now: between nine and ten million workers on strike; no public transportation, no schools, no postal service, no garbage collection; banks, factories, stores closed; electricity comes and goes; no radio and TV except for news.

Here in Spéracèdes the effect of the national strike is slight. There is no mail, no gasoline, no sugar, electrical service is erratic (nothing new)—but life goes on much as usual. We are about four hundred people in Spéracèdes and not that dependent on the outside world. The butcher has his own flock of sheep, most people have their own small farms or gardens. Jeannot and I will plant tomatoes, beans, squash this afternoon. All our friends in Spéracèdes—some of whom, like Jeannot, may be ruined by the strike—are hoping it will continue.

From my window, beyond rows of olive groves, a deep green valley, mountains covered now with broom, red-orange poppies, cypress, the haze has obscured the Mediterranean Sea. (At sunrise, on a clear morning, we see Corsica—150 miles out—from our balcony.) I am on the third floor of our three-room three-storey three-hundred-year-old cottage: with a garden (mimosa, roses, strawberries, parsley, thyme, basil, grapes) it rents for fifty dollars a month. Downstairs Betsey is laboring to make me a birthday cake with the small amount of sugar we have left.

I would like to consider myself radical, revolutionary. I have committed civil disobedience, I have filed a Conscientious Objector's form, I have organized demonstrations, I have taught the poor and the black, I have urged civil disobedience in my writings, I have—like Spock, Goodman, et al—signed complicity statements urging resistance (the first back in 1963), I have sent my draft card back to the government, I have fought against the police—but I have not done what a young man of eighteen or nineteen or twenty does when he sends back his draft card, when he devotes his life to organizing in a ghetto: I have not risked my position and my prospects in my society. After six months in this country village, I feel only the vaguest compulsion to return home, to join the struggle again.

I have begun to try to change my style of living: the possession of property is the beginning of slavery—this is the song Betsey and I sing to one another endlessly. If the government wishes to prosecute me for my numerous illegal acts of resistance, it can—but it's not likely that it will. I'm thirty years old; moreover, the one time I was called for a physical (at the age of twenty-eight, after I'd filed the C. O. form), I was sent home halfway through—high blood pressure.

I don't have high blood pressure. I attributed my score at the Whitehall Induction Center to my paranoia (I was certain they had called me for a physical because I'd told them I would never serve), to the peace buttons I wore on my lapels, to the looks these brought from the military who processed me, to the sight of naked young men, laughing, joking—scared and covering their fright.

The television reports of the revolution here and the memory of the preinduction physical remind me of a French documentary I saw on TV recently. We had been visiting our friends Clément and Fernande Merle (they run the village *Alimentation* and we rent our house from them)—and the documentary was about American soldiers in Vietnam. I remember the sound of a harmonica, a black soldier singing a blues refrain about coming home. I was surprised at how young the soldiers seemed, at how much even the banality of the show could move me. It had been months, I realized, since I'd remembered—with any emotion or feeling—that there was still a war on. None of us said much—but later that evening, for the second time in the six months we've been living here, I was able to get Clément to talk about what life had been like in Spéracèdes during the war: a story about a Jewish family he had hidden out, about the signals the men in Resistance would use to give one another messages in Grasse—something about the way they would fold their newspapers while reading them.

Clément is almost fifty—he calls Betsey and me "mes enfants." Watching the TV documentary, he sighed, closed his eyes, said it again—"Ah, mes enfants . . ." A slight shrug of the shoulders. The TV show disturbed me in a way I was unprepared for: too painful. I wondered again, if—not risking my own life—I had the "right" to demand an end to my government's policies. Seduced by the government line, I suppose—that I am, in some way, letting the boys over there down. The obvious response— that I am *for* American boys, that I am against them being in Vietnam, that I fought to bring them home, to save lives—this now seems mere rhetoric: they are the ones in Vietnam.

Reading Robert Graves's memoir of World War I, *Good-bye to All That*, this week, I typed out a passage. Graves is telling of Siegfried Sassoon's protest against the war, after Sassoon had previously distinguished himself as an almost maniacally heroic soldier. Graves writes—the sentence I copied—that the war's "continuance seemed merely a sacrifice of the idealistic younger generation to the stupidity and self-protective alarm of the elder." Has it ever been different? *Plus ça change . . .*

Here in Spéracèdes, I risk nothing, it seems: neither death nor jail. Betsey and I are pretty sure she's pregnant —we'll know definitely in another week. The doctor (a house and property at the other end of Spéracèdes are given by the village to whatever doctor takes up residence here) says he is "presque certain"—we asked about the possibility of taking a pregnancy test, so that we could be sure, but he discouraged us with a disparaging uplift of the eyebrows—"Les laboratoires, vous savez? . . ." Not wanting to oppose his skepticism concerning French laboratories, or to seem, in some way "typical Americans," we'll wait another week.

Who knows—perhaps if and when I become a father, I will, like friends begin to possess, by instinct, a desire for calm, for stability. I will have, in my bones, a vested interest in the status quo, in protecting what life and property is mine. Who knows? . . . But this is why I am not to be trusted. For no matter what I write, no matter what demonstrations I organize or participate in, no matter how many times I say no to my government—my future—and I cannot say this too many times—is not endangered the way the future of a twenty-year-old is. I have already been twenty, and twenty-one, and twenty-two. I spent those years in nonpolitical activities, and my future is, therefore, barring catastrophe, the unseen, fairly secure. Though I won't court jobs, status, money—they'll probably come in adequate amounts. I'll probably return to America within a year and teach. I enjoy teaching. I'll earn enough money to give us food, clothing, shelter. If my writing sells, I'll have a bit more. If there is political action on my campus, in my city, I know which side I'll be on. True, I am no longer—have not been for some time—in the same left-liberal camp that most of my friends are in. I was aware four and five years ago of the inadequacies of more advertisements by professors, more peace marches, more peace candidates, more antipoverty programs. These were all sops, I said. They all bought off the poor, the protestors. What was needed was a movement which did not request change, but demanded it—and which was prepared to disrupt society, to overthrow the government. I was urging direct action against the war several years back; I found Stokely and Rap and the Black Panthers sensible from the beginning.

Still, I did not need, in my own life, a revolution; I merely wanted one. The difference is crucial. I would like to see a revolution—in my life, in the life of my country, in the world; but I do not, in the conditions of my own material life, need one.

The French seem to need one, and they are getting one. Young people—those I leave behind from this day on —need a revolution. Black people, poor people—they need revolutions because the conditions in which they live—the young, the poor, the black—are, literally, insufferable. They cannot, if they are poor and black, move on, or change—they cannot, as I've done, simply give up America for a year or two. Only if the entire society changes will their lives change. As in France.

But how is this to be done in America? Two dead in a night of riots seems a heavy toll in France. Thirty or forty dead in rioting in a single American city seems part of the order of things. Item in the *International Herald Tribune*, dateline Washington, April 24:

> Forty-six persons were killed in the disorders that erupted after the murder of the Rev. Dr. Martin Luther King Jr. April 4, Justice Department figures showed yesterday.
>
> The compilation, based on reports from 76 cities, also listed a total of 2,561 persons injured and 28,271 arrested.
>
> The 46 deaths occurred in 13 cities. That nationwide figure compared with 43 deaths in Detroit last July, 23 deaths in the Newark riots, also last July, and 34 persons killed in the Watts district of Los Angeles in August, 1965.

This way of describing reality comes as naturally as the gathering of the data. America seems too rich, too powerful, too well insulated to fall at once, to be changed by a few days or years of riots.

The young, the black—they have neither the numbers nor the power nor the skill in the exercise of what power they have to shut down, to threaten the entire nation. Can there be a revolution, peaceful or otherwise, without the support of workers? The young, the black, their numbers insufficient to date, need the support of the workers, but in America this is the last segment of society from which they will ever receive support. From that underclass of workers—the one below organized labor—yes; but from organized labor, never. What many of my liberal friends said to my arguments for revolution before I left: that America was big enough and flexible enough to absorb change and cataclysm, seems true. Not in the way one finds liberals rushing headlong to approve and embrace this fact (e.g., Irving Howe in an article in *The New York Review of Books*, praising Eugene McCarthy's presidential campaign: "For all its creakiness and cumbersomeness, the democratic process seems to have come through pretty damned well."), but simply as a description of the way things are. Reassuring to the majority, I suppose.

Time, in its coverage of the national strike here, compares the French and American systems. *Time*'s position (whatever is, in America, is right) is brilliantly phrased; it would, alas, probably be endorsed not only by the likes of Lyndon Johnson and Barry Goldwater, but by everybody this side of what *Time* labels The New Left: McCarthy, labor unions, ADA, NAACP, *Dissent* magazine:

> In the U. S., where power is widely diffused, serious dissatisfaction with policies, politicians or insti-

tutions can be resolved or at least ameliorated by
democratic processes—despite the extremist assertion that "the system" is hopeless. Unlike French
workers and students, most Americans with a cause
can lodge their protest with the hope of inducing
reasonable change by their numbers and their voices
rather than by entirely rebuilding society or bringing down an elected government between elections.

There has been no clearer, more honest statement of
the American Myth. Either you believe in it, or you
don't. Either you think that solutions to problems are
forthcoming through such a system, or you don't.

If it need be said again—I might *wish* that the above
description of things were truthful and adequate—but it
is not: moreover, I realize, I've come to believe that the
maintenance of this myth actually impedes necessary
change. The illusion is maintained that such change is
possible within the political process, when this isn't so.
While the basic structure of the society remains intact,
the myth forces critics to limit the fire of their protests,
their demands. It reserves all power to the system. The
price we pay for democracy, then, is to lose our freedom.
No paradox. Power is so diffused in America, as *Time*
notes, that it is held by those who would prevent change
—i.e., by the majority. Whether in their own best or worst
interests, we shall see. What is certain is that the causes
of the war in Vietnam and the murder of King are too per-
vasive, too deep, to be dealt with by the policies available.

According to the newspaper which I saw in the *bistro* this morning, the NLF has launched its third major
attack of the year against Saigon. The day the Tet offensive began I met a friend at the Nice airport: a middle-
aged American writer. Also there to meet him, a well-
known American writer, one who has written many

political essays, books—the word "radical" prominent in the title of one. Both of them were upset, worried by the Tet offensive, by the possibility of an NLF victory. It might mean, they explained, the resurgence of McCarthyism in America. So strange to me to have the events in Vietnam prove their significance in this way: I was not old enough, I suppose, to have suffered this legacy of McCarthyism. The liberal's credo—*all* must take second place to the preservation of civil liberties in America; anything that threatens to destroy them must be opposed. More important to preserve free speech than to resist genocide. This is what they say, by what they do.

Time is easy here. Even a national strike—a revolution—does not disturb the essential tranquility of life. We rise early, I walk into town to get the day's bread (fresh, warm), we eat—then I go upstairs to write and Betsey goes downstairs—or outside—to paint. (Our bathroom—next to her "studio"—used to be the chicken coop.) Toward noon Betsey begins to make lunch, and when I'm finished with my morning's work, I join her in the kitchen—I read her what I've written, she shows me her painting, then I help her prepare our meal. We eat slowly, leisurely—entrée, main dish, vegetable, salad, cheese, fruit, wine. On warm days we move our table onto the balcony. Our lunch hour lasts until two or three o'clock. After, we usually take a long walk, visit with friends, read (we've both been going through mammoth nineteenth-century novels by Dickens, Eliot, Tolstoy— books we'd never found time for in America), finish up our morning's work, take naps, talk. We have a late supper—usually at about eight o'clock—of soup, cheese, and fruit—and, on the nights we don't visit with friends, we read together in bed. . . . America grows further and further away. We're rarely homesick for our country, or for any part of it—not even for friends and family.

I enjoy my garden, I enjoy not having to do anything at any particular time, I enjoy being able to spend
twenty-four hours a day with Betsey. To my surprise, I
get on well without a telephone, and without numerous
other things: without television and sports (I used to
sit through two or three football games in a row on TV
every Saturday and Sunday), without washing machines
and dryers, dry cleaning, supermarkets, electrical appli-
ances, central heating, political activities. Reassuring to
confirm what I've wanted to believe: that I could get
along without the conveniences of modern society. For
much of the time we even get along without a refrigerator. The one Clément gave us is a tiny two-shelf ancient
Frigidaire, "Made in USA"; its motor, however, comes
from an oversized French refrigerator, so that for at least
twelve hours every day we have to keep the plug out of
the socket. Even when it works, Betsey sometimes finds it
easier to leave the plug out all the time. Like much of
Clément's handy work—as our friend Jacques has pointed
out—it is a perfect example of French *bricolage*—
"définitif-provisoire."

The most amazing thing for me during the past two
weeks is that I discovered I could live without mail. I
never would have thought it possible. I've always doted
on mail—at least from the time eleven years ago when I
sent out my first novel. During the first few months here
I'd always found an excuse to make a second trip to the
post office (mail is picked up every morning at nine by
most villagers), just in case Georgette, the postmistress,
had put a letter of mine in somebody else's stack. (In
Spéracèdes, you can buy stamps and make calls on credit
—Georgette keeps a record of the town's debts to the
P.T.T. in a narrow-lined school copybook.) About two
years ago I had the dream of dreams: I went to my mailbox, opened it, took out a pile of twenty or thirty letters,

and the mailbox was filled again. The process repeated itself endlessly. I woke up smiling: I had seen Paradise.

My politics grow more radical, my temperament mellows. Life here, hopefully, has unfitted me for a return to American civilization. It's not so difficult to give up the American way of life when one can replace it with something more satisfying. Food, clothing, shelter, work one loves, friends one can see often—what more does a man need?

I wonder if black revolutionaries will ever renounce their claims on the cities—of what use can these polluted accumulations of steel and concrete be to human beings? The cities are dead, incapable of renewal. To struggle, to risk life, to die—in order to control Manhattan Island or Los Angeles? . . . There must be other possibilities.

In Grasse, the farmers and merchants have been giving food to the workers, free. In Paris, students have been giving away chickens. As often in such crises (cf. the New York subway strikes, blackout)—a certain release of inhibition, a lifting of repressions . . .

The students have been buoyant, joyful. They went into the streets, battled with police, and the workers—to everybody's surprise (including that of the students)—joined them. When Prime Minister Pompidou offered amnesty, reopening of the Sorbonne, withdrawal of police, and promise of reform, the students responded by occupying the university. They took over the Odéon, where they are still camped, engaging in continuous dialogue. "When the General Assembly becomes a bourgeois theater," one of their signs reads, "bourgeois theater must become the General Assembly." When Daniel Cohn-Bendit was asked, in a TV interview, why he wasn't satisfied with the government's concessions, his reply was direct, simple: "Because nothing has changed." Not only the university, but the society which is reflected in the antiquated structure of the university must change, and change radically.

The workers seem to agree. Despite the fact that the government—and, more important, the French Communist Party and the Communist-dominated C. G. T. (Confédération Générale du Travail—the largest French labor union)—have been steadily attacking and maligning the students (the Communist Party has called them "provocateurs," "counterrevolutionaries," "poor little rich boys"), the workers have maintained their alliance with the students. Moreover, the workers have rejected the strike-breaking offers made to them by the government and private companies—offers which their own leadership had recommended they accept. The offers seemed considerable—a 10 percent raise in all salaries, more social security benefits, a reduction of the workweek to forty hours, a raise in the minimum hourly wage (to sixty cents an hour)—but the workers voted the package down and they continue to occupy the factories, demanding for themselves what the students have demanded: substantial control of the processes (of management) which govern their lives.

If, here in France, or in Czechoslovakia, Spain, West Germany, the students seem united in their opposition to the government (whether it be Communist, Fascist, or Democratic), in America the radical students remain, distinctly, a minority. Most students, like most Americans, guard their positions and prospects. The numbers of radicals grow, the power of students to disrupt society, to control their immediate environments (e.g., Berkeley, Columbia) grows also—but this has no decisive effect on the society beyond university walls. The effect of student rebellions is buffered all along the line, reforms are (sometimes) instituted, things return to normal, life goes on as usual. The ordinary processes of life are not interrupted or changed for significant numbers of people.

Something else should be said: it is natural for young people to change their style of living and risk everything. The world has gone wrong, America is sick, things must be transformed, revolution is the order of the day: one has, if he perceives the world this way, no choice but to drop out, to turn one's energies to resistance, revolution, reconstruction. Is it another thing for me to reject the world that I have accepted, if partially, these thirty years? I like to think so; this would be—from habit—unnatural.

In fact, I don't know how it's done. How does one give up the American way of life and still remain in America? If one feels the necessity to be involved in the struggle for radical change, then one must remain in America. But what then? Some over thirty will, as I will, give support, will be arrested (jail seems the risk we run nowadays to allow our consciences to continue to function on American soil), will get their heads cracked—but their lives will like mine remain, generally, middle-class American. The revolution that will change the order of things will come from without, if it comes at all.

What is the good of withholding a percentage of one's income tax, for example, or all of it, if, with the money one earns, one remains a contributing member of the society? Those, for example, who refuse to buy Volkswagens or to invest in Chase Manhattan or First National City Banks should, by this logic, refuse to buy the products of *any* American corporation. But one cannot be part of a society—even for the purposes of revolution—and exist outside it. The center of day-to-day living is undramatic, a series of compromises. The center of revolution, also, is undramatic—not one confrontation after another with state troopers, not meetings in dingy base-ments with African chieftains, not warehouses of arms and battle plans; but, more simply, essentially: organizing people where they are so that they can seize control of those things which affect their lives.

In the end, as always, one does the best one can. For the past few months I've been writing about the period of time I spent, at twenty-two, as a junior executive for the General Motors Corporation—and of the ways this experience affected me personally, politically. Several months ago I would have tried to justify the fact of my writing about GM, about politics. Now I don't. The political for me seems endlessly bound with the personal. This doesn't invalidate political commitment, but it does lead me away from issuing calls to revolution, from attempting purely political analyses, from prophesying.

Walk yesterday afternoon with Betsey, picking wildflowers. Incredible reds, yellows, violets. Olive trees are being uprooted near the town cemetery two hundred yards from our house. The cemetery is being enlarged. The trees are dug out and encased in wood slats, the roots and earth bound round in metal, like huge tubs. We collect wood scraps to use for making buttons, knick-knacks. Graves, in his description of trench warfare:

> The trenches were wide and tumble-down, too shallow in many places, and without sufficient traverses. The French had left relics both of their nonchalance—corpses buried too near the surface; and of their love of security—a number of deep though lousy dug-outs.

My impulse, when I sometimes think of returning to America: to buy a home in the woods, to stock in food, books, to tend to my garden, to avoid contact with cities; in a society which continuously assaults one with the need to aggrandize possessions, property, power—which, in its everlasting Puritanism, still regards the lack of these

things as the proof of Sin—is it surprising that some men
should try to steal the power of others by taking their
lives? I used to wonder, in California, when some enraged student was going to take a shot at me while I delivered an antiwar speech. But to kill me he would have
to have identified with me . . .

Even a trip to *Monoprix* (a combination supermar-
ket-department store the size of a small Woolworth's), in
Grasse, has become too much for me. The sight of men
and women standing in lines at checkout counters, not
speaking to one another or to the cashiers, their arms
laden with groceries (there are no shopping carts yet,
only plastic handbaskets) seems absurd, insane, unnatural. One of my daily pleasures, I know, is talking with
Clément and Fernande when I buy our groceries and
vegetables. Romantic, of course, but it no longer seems to
me unrealistic to believe that the purchase of one's food
—like the cooking of it, the eating—should, in some way,
be human and pleasurable—part of the daily round of
one's life.

Perhaps the reason I find myself responding so instinctively, so positively, to the actions of the students
here is because I find that I agree with them about the
nature of the enemy—which is not merely the archaic
university and its structure, not merely the de Gaulle re-
gime, not merely—not *even* such things as imperialism,
fascism, capitalism, communism, bureaucracy, mech-
anization—but something more general and generalized,
more comprehensive and lethal: *la société de consommation*—the consumer society. (Sign on the Sorbonne:
"Commodities are the opium of the people.")

My feeling—unprovable, of course—is that America
will tolerate anything except an assault on its consumer
culture. It will tolerate riots in the schools, riots in the

ghettos, riots in the cities—but when the disruption threatens to move into the shopping centers, the supermarkets, the department stores, and the factories which create the commodities—then the nation will move, act, repress, and do everything necessary to preserve its "freedom of choice," its right to buy and consume an expanding quantity of goods at an expanding rate.

In the local stores we receive credit until the banks open again. In Spéracèdes people have not, as they have in the cities, ransacked the shelves. (Fernande Merle rations sugar.) One reason things have moved so quickly, everybody agrees, is that Paris is at the heart of things. (One could, conceivably, shut down a half-dozen major American cities and life would go on normally in the rest of America.) If you close down Paris you close down France. Not long ago all produce—even from this region (the south)—would go north to Paris before being redistributed southward. Though they worship bureaucracy, the French are not masters at organization. Everybody laughs at the quality of mass-produced goods here. Jacqueline claims that, even on an assembly line, a French worker retains his individualism: you cannot, quite simply, tell him to do something a certain way—the way you want everyone to—and expect him to follow instructions. He will nod, shrug, and do it the way he wants. Although the French changed their currency officially from "old" to "new" francs ten years ago (100 old francs became one new franc; one new franc equals 100 centimes), most Frenchmen still calculate only in old francs. In newspapers, two prices are listed for most items. On such a base of character, you do not build an efficient new order.

Nor do you build a thriving industrial economy. Despite de Gaulle, France has been hurting economically. The average French worker now earns between $150 and

$170 per month, though the wages vary from region to region, higher in Paris (around $200), lower here ($100), where there is much cheap Algerian and Spanish labor. Unemployment and prices have been rising (a Frenchman spends at least half his salary on food, not only because he loves to eat, but because most meat and canned goods are about twice the price of comparable American food; gasoline is over eighty cents a gallon). Businesses have been failing (virtually all the local perfume factories in Grasse—five miles away—have been bought by American companies). And in de Gaulle's Common Market, French goods have a hard time competing against German and Dutch ones. At the same time, the French worker is made to feel inferior because he cannot become part of the new consumer culture (there are witty thirty-second ads on TV, one after the other, on how to use the bank, how to use aluminum foil, how to use electrical appliances, how to be a "modern" housewife, how to obtain credit; there are no ads for private companies, for brand names: the ads, then, are parodies of American commercials; appeals, simply, to consume—food, perfume, leather, automobiles, wristwatches, etc.). It's not surprising that the government's appeals to end the strike because it is hurting the ordinary man (Pompidou pleading last night for a return to "la vie normale") go unheeded.

There are demonstrations every day in all major cities (Spéracèdes was to have one last night, but the rain washed the notice, written in chalk, from the wall of the *mairie*.) The continuing unrest in the country is due in large part to the action of the de Gaulle government, forbidding Daniel Cohn-Bendit to return to France from Germany, where he was speaking to students. This brought the students back into the streets after several days marked by a lack of confrontation between them and the police. Two nights of pitched battle followed, the students setting up barricades in the Latin Quarter—from overturned cars, bricks pried from the street, debris, gratings, trees, garbage cans. Even *Time* Magazine was shocked by the brutality of the French police (e.g., taking people out of ambulances to beat them up), an indication of the ferocity of the combat. The students, despite the intensity of the battles, still refuse to play things according to the usual script. After Cohn-Bendit had secretly made his way back into France, his organization (The Movement of March 22nd, named for the day the students first occupied the University at Nanterre) called a press conference. The reporters showed up to interview Cohn-Bendit. They were met by other student leaders, who stated, smiling: *"We* are Dany." ("The great danger," Cohn-Bendit said this week, "lies in a revolutionary movement which tends to become just another show for our consumer society."—"un autre spectacle pour notre société de consommation.")

The government's hope (implicit in its action against Cohn-Bendit) that the workers and students would divide and fight one another has proven to be true (thanks largely to the Communist Party)—but not true enough. Pierre Mendès-France marched with the students two days ago, though the Communist Party and the C. G. T. refused to. Note well, though: in the first night following Cohn-Bendit's banishment, more than half of those arrested were young workers, many of them unemployed.

Odors drift up from the kitchen, pleasant. The sun wavers—sometimes out, sometimes in—and I can see the vague line of the horizon, of the sea. Betsey and I will stand on the balcony for hours at a time sometimes, especially toward evening, watching the changing effects of the light, the wind, the sun. Friends are coming to visit this afternoon, to have lunch with us: we'll talk, eat, have birthday cake, I'll do some gardening with Jeannot, the day will pass, I'll continue on the book I'm writing. In about a year I'll probably return to America. I will return believing what I believed eight years ago, when I was a junior executive trainee at General Motors: that the only hope—for the world, for myself—is immediate revolution. I won't, as I did then, feel that I am one of the agents that can bring it about, or that we will all die within six months if it is not brought about. I will be resigned: if the Vietnam war is (hopefully) over by then, it will only mean that the long-range, day-to-day and undramatic work can begin—attacking those things, deep in our way of life, of which Vietnam is only the most spectacular and cruel symptom.

Here in Spéracèdes I find myself becoming more and more direct with others, and perhaps this too is a function of becoming thirty years old. Life seems too short for lies, too short for living as one does not wish to—so I do what I want: the things that are most important to me, to separate the inseparable, are three: my writing, politics, my life with my wife and my friends.

Maybe you can't trust people over thirty because they know they're going to die. When I was eighteen, at the end of my second year of college, I was operated on for a small tumor: the doctors and my family feared cancer, I was radiated afterwards. Walking from St. Luke's Hospital the afternoon the doctor had asked me to come to the hospital for a biopsy, I felt good: the first thought that came to mind, after the thought that I might die within the year, was that I would not have to finish a term paper for a literature course.

One is never aware of all the defense mechanisms at one's disposal; still, the thoughts which followed were that I would be more attractive, mysterious to girls, I would be able to write a great novel, I would be able to do what I wanted for a year, I would receive endless

sympathy—and endless adulation for not appearing to
want any . . .

Notice of death at this point would not be so welcome: it would produce, I imagine, neither grandiosity
nor relief. I like to think I'd react the way Orwell did
during the Spanish Civil War. In his report on the war,
Homage to Catalonia, he describes what went through
his mind after he'd been shot through the neck. "There
must have been about two minutes in which I assumed
that I was killed. . . . My first thought, conventionally,
was for my wife. My second was a violent resentment at
having to leave this world which, when all is said and
done, suits me so well."

Perhaps then, if one has this sense of mortality, one
becomes, in one's own life, that deadliest of things: responsible. But if one risks his life anyway, I'd like to think
he risks more—for he knows what he is giving up, he has
been to places that those who begin as revolutionaries at
nineteen or twenty have never seen.

Yet without the recklessness of youth, it becomes difficult to risk much; one values too many things. I am too
aware, for example, of the actual (though partial) good
that certain programs do for individuals to be able, in the
hopes of getting the kinds of programs which would help
all people, to reject the inadequate programs totally. And
I am too aware, today, of the actual hardship the national
strike is imposing on many to desire, in all my feelings,
that it go on very much longer. I know it has to go on
longer if there's to be any hope for the changes I want
. . . but I can't look forward to it.

I remember, when I was teaching at Columbia in
1964, a discussion with another young teacher, one who
described himself as a Marxist-Leninist. We were talking
about Vietnam and I was lamenting the deaths of civil-
ians, including those killed by the NLF. His reaction was

a scornful "You can't have an omelet without breaking some eggs." This cowed me, made me feel inadequate, confused. I wondered if I could ever be a "true revolutionary."

It occurs to me that I am, technically, liable to at least five years in jail for having urged resistance, for having sent back my draft card. That should—however remote—be faced. My immediate reaction: I would not endure five years in jail, I'd return to Spéracèdes. This then, may be the best reason for not trusting me now that I am thirty; for just as Huck lost interest in "Moses and the Bulrushers" when he found out that they had lived thousands of years ago ("I don't take no stock in dead people"), I'd probably lose interest in political action, at this point in my life, if it meant five years in jail. I don't take much stock in jail—not for me, not now: America doesn't seem worth it.

Yet my mind engages in a mad political calculus— five years never, four no, three probably not, but if the sentence were a year, even two—all right, then, I'd go: the political value might compensate. This, despite the fact that I regard all court battles as somewhat irrelevant; opportunities not so much to radicalize America as to vindicate, to justify the American system (which allows free speech, due process, legal battles over resistance, during wartime). What it would be, if the time came, is a question of tactics, of weighing possibilities. Like most Americans, I'd have to ask the pragmatic question: *How much good would it do?*

A true revolutionary (my romantic version of one?), if he dies during a revolution, does not die knowing—or even hoping—that his death is necessary to overthrow the forces of oppression. He dies because he dies; he dies for the revolution, to be sure, but he dies because he has no choice; he does not ask if his death "will do good," if it will "accomplish something." For five years of prison I'd probably have to have the reassurance I wouldn't need for my other actions: that it would do more good, in some tangible way, for society, for others, than it would do harm to me. Unproductive self-sacrifice, martyrdom—they don't interest me.

I feel at peace today. Unusually so. There will be many days, soon, as there have been recently, when my rage against all that I find wrong with the world, against my country, against individuals, against all the murder, hunger, the grinding down of lives—will rise up in me so that I feel ready to do whatever is necessary—without hope of success—to change things. To murder, to give up my family, my writing, my own life . . .

But one must, so they say, be realistic. Changes take time (though those who say this can well afford, it always seems, to wait; those they urge patience on cannot). But bitterness, rage, sorrow—the emotions that I refer to lately as my political emotions—they come and go. What matters is the commitment which resides. I am thirty years old today. I might wish that all human beings could have certain things—I think of the final scene in *Figaro*, when, after the masks have been taken off, the lovers revealed to one another, the men forgiven by their mistresses, all join, happily, gloriously in song: *tutti contenti saremo cosi* (Let us all be happy together, forever, as we are now). But my reference, a musical-literary one, is the giveaway. The world is not about to turn into a Mozart opera; idyllic desires for peace, for justice, for the ability of human beings to do what they want with their lives, to love one another, etcetera, etcetera—such desires, translated into expository prose, remain as vague and abstract as the speeches of those I would tumble from power. Everybody wants peace, everybody wants happiness for mankind, goodwill between all men: but everybody does not want revolution, will not take the risks, will not make the commitments with their own lives that revolution will require.

Still, peaceful today, enraged tomorrow, my life has changed. The emotions, thoughts which came to life during my stay at General Motors eight years ago have proven more powerful than I suspected. I've been rereading things I wrote at the time, and I laugh at myself for certain ways of saying and seeing that I hope I've outgrown—but I do not deny what I saw and said: without revolution, America is doomed.

A month ago nobody could have predicted what is happening in France today. Still, I don't expect that the conditions which produced this revolution will occur in America. I do whatever I do without illusion—what I and those I want to work with are struggling for is not about to be achieved—perhaps not in our lifetimes, perhaps never. But the movement we build, if built well, is the only hope we have; the only way we know, now, to begin to obtain and exert power, to begin to control our lives, to begin to give up what must be given up, to create what must be created, to risk what must be risked.

If I'm out of the country for a year or two or three, and if I feel, as I apparently do, a need to justify my absence, I can reassure myself with the thought that there will be more than enough work to do when I return.

On the front page of the *Nice-Matin*, the local paper (pages two and three detail automobile accidents, robberies, weddings, births, murders, suicides), is an item that draws me back to America: THREE YEARS IN PRISON FOR THE HUSBAND OF JOAN BAEZ. I worked with Dave Harris last year—he was organizing the Resistance on the West Coast at the time I was organizing faculty and others for civil disobedience against the war; we gave speeches from the same platforms, helped organize the Oakland Induction Center action of October 16, 1967, etc.

Thought: the logic of events continues to confirm the notion of an "historical force"—the Vietnam war and the events that have been attached to it continue to make Marxists of many of us (without, like myself, bothering or needing to read Marx). Dave changed the Stanford campus (he was president of the student body)—one of the best public speakers I've ever heard: charismatic, especially for those of high school age. And though the faculty at Stanford had not been apathetic before I came there, I did organize them on a new level of involvement, action. (The call to civil disobedience issued by forty-seven of the faculty last May, which I initiated, was brought East by Mitchell Goodman—teaching at Stanford in the spring—and became the basis for organizing the Justice Department confrontation which led to the Spock trial.) Still, history moves without us—this year, when Dave, Mitch, and I are gone from the campus, Stanford had its most militant actions—burning down an ROTC building, occupying campus buildings for several days, winning major concessions from the administration. Last year when we marched on the Stanford Research Institute, a corporation involved in chemical and biological warfare research, we were able to rouse only fifty students, three faculty members.

Curious irony: after my journey these last eight years, my increasing politicalization and radicalization, I found I had left America just before the start of its most turbulent year: the growth of the Resistance, the Oakland demonstration, the battle of the Pentagon, Johnson's decision to retire, the murder of King and the ensuing ghetto riots, the ascendancy of Black Power, the ascendancy of Student Power, including, prominently, its rise at two universities (Columbia, Stanford) I'd taught at the last three years. I exchanged that for the peace and quiet of southern France, only to find myself living in the midst of revolution. Which suggests that what has gone on here for over two weeks now, initiated by the students (n.b., less than 10 percent of the students in France come from working-class families), is not about to end. The most significant upheaval is occurring here, but the forces that generated it are felt everywhere. My guess (I'm not alone, of course) is that 1968 is a turning point—much that will happen during the next generation will seem to stem directly from events of this year. And what happens here, in Germany, in Czechoslovakia, in America, is all of a piece. Put most simply, it is the struggle of the young against the old: not merely their disavowal of the ideological and power politics of the Cold War, but their refusal to be part of the bourgeois-technological society that has been offered to them as the reward for political and moral acquiescence. They will not, in simplest terms, be part of a world which does not make sense to them. The signs the students in Paris have been posting tell the story; this one in the Sorbonne amphitheater: "I take my desires for reality because I believe in the reality of my desires." Another, less abstract: "Humanity will only be happy when the last capitalist is strangled with the guts of the last bureaucrat." Though, at present, the struggle is a political one, the minds of the students are fixed on things that go beyond political struggle. In their version of things there is an end both to ideology *and* to politics. They raise the black flag, not the red. (On the door of the Sorbonne, May 13: "The revolution which is beginning will call in question not only capitalist society but industrial society. The consumer society is bound for a violent death. Social alienation must vanish from history. We are inventing a new and original world. Imagination is seizing power.")

In Paris, de Gaulle appeals for unity in the face of a

"Communist menace"; he appeals for the "preservation of law," for the "voice of democracy" (via new elections); at the same time he lets it be known that he has met with General Jacques Massu, the commander of all French forces in Germany, that Army units (with tanks) are on the outskirts of Paris, that reservists have been called up.

The Communist Party quickly reinforces de Gaulle's appeal by endorsing his call for new elections, by condemning militant student groups, by continuing to urge its members to boycott the student demonstrations "in order not to provoke further incidents." After de Gaulle's speech, we take a quick trip into Grasse, in Jacques's car, to the *bourse du travail* of the C. G. T. A handful of workers, all of them depressed. One whispers to us that "they are ready to fight the police." But Jacques laughs and notes that the worker has only five sad-faced men with him. (On my first full day in Spéracèdes, I remember, Jacques and I got into a long political discussion. I was a bit puzzled by the fact that, though our village was traditionally Communist, all the Communists—such as the Merles—seemed to be quite capitalist in their accumulation of property. "Ah," Jacques said, and he proceeded to give me one of his special definitions, "un communiste français, vous savez, c'est quelqu'un qui veut la grande voiture de son voisin."—"A French Communist, you see, is someone who wants to own his neighbor's big car.")

In Texas, Lyndon Johnson states at a press conference that he would prefer "not to comment on the decisions" taken by the French government, but he adds that it is "very important to the American people and for the rest of the world that we have stability in France." I note the possessive pronoun.

Our friends all spent the afternoon here: they brought presents, we ate cake, sang songs, I delivered a discourse from our balcony to the assembly in our garden, we played *yan* with dice, we listened to the radio. Good to share this kind of life with friends one cares about; in a community that can be traversed by foot. What Sapir was writing about over forty years ago—the almost psychotic split in our industrial civilization between work and pleasure—is crucial. Men cannot work eight hours a day at tasks unfit for human beings, and become human beings in the time that remains: what I sensed at GM. But it is worse in America, because American workers get well paid for their assembly-line work, and thus believe more in its necessity, its benevolence.

When the French workers can fully enter the consumer society most differences will be gone. What seems so unique about our life in Spéracèdes is not only that there is no dividing line between our work and our pleasure (I would write, Betsey would paint, I would raise food even if I received economic sustenance from other sources), but that no part of our life seems compartmentalized. Not even visiting with friends. To visit is a natural part of the daily process, as writing is. For us, as for the others here, existence has not been segmented, organized: three hours for work, two hours for recreation, two evenings for entertainment. Within ten minutes walking time we can take care of all our needs, see all our friends. Our activities flow into one another as the days do: without any sense of time being divided. Our friends work in their own homes (writing, silkscreening, painting, selling groceries, making wine, raising jasmine, doing ceramic work, graphics, etc.), so that even that division is eliminated—like our friends, we don't leave home for work: we live where we work, we work as we live.

Thirty years old on the thirtieth day of the month; the memorial day for the dead of past wars, the day of de

Gaulle's speech, the day I cease to be trustworthy. If de Gaulle had resigned the day would have been perfect. As usual, I have been too optimistic. The workers will hold out if they can hold out. The readiness is all. As always. All that matters is what happens. Intentions, hopes, reasons, "almosts," "ifs"—all irrelevant. For me, for everyone, all that matters are outward events. From *The Ethics of the Fathers:* "Who is the righteous man? He who does righteous deeds."

We could, I suppose, organize inside the prisons . . .

. . . But for what? As soon as the words are down I sense that they are false, that they derive not from what I feel now, but from habit, from some reflex action, from an impulse that dies hard, if at all: the desire to end on a note of hope, to find a way to blend somehow, in positive terms, the moral and the political, to promise an action which, if only in rhetoric, forges a political program from a virtuous gesture. Prison would be an indulgence, a waste. Spéracèdes is better.

I wrote almost all of the above in one sitting—the greatest quantity of first-draft writing I'd ever done in my life. I felt high when I finished, and all afternoon I unwound, repeating—for myself, for our friends—the fact: thirty pages on the thirtieth day of the month of my thirtieth year. Except for the temporary malaise caused by de Gaulle's speech (since there was no electricity, Jacques listened with a weak transistor radio to one ear, repeating —with groans and curses—the General's speech), we were all in good spirits. While I delivered my birthday speech from our balcony, our friends raised our own flag in the garden below—my long underwear. During the week which followed, I continued to keep a journal—no more than a page or two a day—and I've incorporated a few paragraphs of that journal in the preceding section.

Exactly one week after my thirtieth birthday—on June 6th—I stopped keeping the journal. The convergence of events that day was too much: the anniversary of VE Day, the day the national strike ended officially, the day Robert Kennedy was assassinated, the day—that afternoon, about five hours after we'd heard the news about Kennedy—that Doctor Joussaume told us what we'd expected to hear: Betsey was pregnant.

Though I no longer agree with many of the things I wrote that week, though as I reread I want to correct, qualify, modify, delete, update—I've made only minor revisions, none of them substantive. The thoughts that spilled so easily represent one end of a journey I'd been on since, at least, my days at GM—and they represent—by their tone as much as by anything I actually said—thoughts, feelings—a mood—which had been gathering in me, had been with me for some time before my thirtieth birthday.

We had been living in Spéracèdes for slightly more than six months when my thirtieth birthday arrived, and though I've left my brief description of our life there as I wrote it then, I should add one note: our life in Spéracèdes was neither ideal nor idyllic; it was good. The difference is important.

It was good, not because Spéracèdes was in France, not because we lived in a three-hundred-year-old house and saw the Mediterranean Sea and the Esterel mountains from our balcony, not because we ate luxurious midday two- and three-hour meals, not because we were both working steadily and well at things we loved (though such things—to put it mildly—helped). It was good not only because the rhythm of our daily life seemed whole

and natural, not only because we were spared some of
the more brutal products and byproducts of the modern
world; not—in short—because (as I may have given the
impression) we had, in a village where the women still
washed their clothes in the fountain in the town square,
returned to some kind of idyllic pastoral or preindustrial
life. Our life in Spéracèdes was good because—or so it
seems now—we had good friends and we could see them
every day if we wanted to. Like ourselves, they worked
mostly at home, and, like ourselves, they were always
ready and able to spend unlimited amounts of time with
us, with one another.

Our house, our village, the sea, the food—we loved
these things (in a country where most cuts of meat ran
close to two dollars a pound, we quickly—and painlessly
—adapted ourselves to a diet which had as its staples
wine, bread, and cheese)—but they seem somewhat irrelevant to our life there. What matters is that, for a year
and a half, Betsey and I were able to spend twenty-four
hours a day together, day after day—and for a year and a
half we were able to spend as much time as we wanted
with—the phrase cannot be changed—people we loved.

There were, for most of our time in Spéracèdes, eight
families in what we called "la groupe" (or "la troupe")—
only half of whom had been there when we arrived in December, 1967. We respected one another's privacy almost
religiously (when Jacques was in a bad mood we might not
see him for four or five days), and, at the same time, felt
part of a community, felt that all our friends' houses were
always open to us.

After lunch, if Betsey and I would stop by a friend's
house, we might sit there with them, talking, while they
continued to do their work (silkscreening, making lampshades, painting)—and sometimes we would find ourselves there, still talking, at midnight. Not so unusual, of

course: but what seems remarkable now is that this happened regularly, and that it seemed normal, natural.

If I finished my work early in the morning—before noon—I knew I could always find a group of friends in the *bistro;* they'd stop there for an apéritif before lunch (we were the only family still without children; our friends' children would pass by on the way home from school—the lunch hour for Spéracèdes' two-room schoolhouse lasted from 11:30 to 1:30)—and sometimes we'd wind up eating lunch in the *bistro* (*baguettes, paté, saucisson,* fruit, cheese), and then spending the rest of the day (and evening) together.

We didn't always talk. In fact, for the first time in my life, I was able to sit in a room with friends—none of us saying anything—and not mind the silence. In the childhood and adolescence of my own Brooklyn-Jewish home, or during evenings spent—in New York, Bloomington, Palo Alto—with friends, I had, instinctively, always felt uncomfortable—had always assumed something was *wrong* if nobody was speaking. Silence was hostility.

Betsey and I could spend two or three hours together in our kitchen—preparing a meal, eating it—without saying a word, and without, we would realize afterwards, minding the fact. (Though Betsey—she'd grown up in a small Indiana town—had never minded silence, had always been somewhat overwhelmed by the verbosity of my New York family and friends.) The same with friends: we enjoyed spending time with those people in whose physical presence we felt good, at ease, comfortable (a person's most important quality, we all agreed, was that he or she be *ouvert*—open, unguarded, direct, vulnerable)—not with those who, by their ideas or achievements, were "interesting."

What made our life especially rich, though, was that our friends were—*even* in their ideas and work—more than interesting; and it was chance (*bonne chance*) which brought us all to Spéracèdes at the same time.

Nancy Cusack and her husband Ralph had settled there fifteen years before we arrived—they had had to leave Ireland and settle in a Mediterranean climate because of Ralph's health—and they had bought a small farm on one edge of the village, where they raised jasmine (for selling to the perfume factories in Grasse), grapes (for making their own wine), fruit and vegetables (for themselves). Ralph had been a well-known painter in Ireland, a novelist (*Cadenza*—published in England and America), and a journalist (for *The Irish Times*)—and he and Nancy had been in business together in Ireland, selling bulbs for wildflowers. Ralph had died two years before we arrived in Spéracèdes, and Nancy continued to take care of the farm with the help of the five Cusack children (ages fifteen to thirty). By about our third month in Spéracèdes, Betsey and I were seeing Nancy every day; when our own house was rented for July and August, we lived with her for almost a month, camped under an apricot tree.

It was in her kitchen more than in any other place in Spéracèdes that I felt at home, at peace. Every afternoon during the school year, toward five, when Nancy's youngest daughter, Annabel, would arrive from the *lycée* in Grasse, Nancy would serve tea and hot currant bread which she made from sour milk. Her kitchen was always full, overflowing—cats, kittens, paintings, books, baskets of fruit, clothes for washing, pots and bottles of jams and preserves, tables overrun with dishes, cloth napkins, magazines, bowls of old bread (we kept the old bread we didn't use for our own breadcrumbs, stuffing, and *soupe à l'oignon* in a cloth sack and brought it to Nancy when it was full; she made a mush with it which she fed to her chickens), records, music scores (Nancy was a fine cellist and every summer and Easter, when her brother and sister-in-law visited from Geneva, they would play piano-violin-cello trios together), the day's meals, and dirty dishes. There were rarely less than seven or eight for tea.

Although we saw Nancy every day—and talked endlessly (about cooking, food, books, music, art, Spéracèdes, Ireland)—it was at least six months before we realized that her cousin Sam in Paris, from whom she'd receive notes from time to time, was Sam Beckett. And it was not until shortly before we left Spéracèdes for a 9,000-mile camping trip (at the end of July) that she referred at all to her childhood in Dublin—to family friends such as W. B. and Jack Yeats, James Joyce (who was always borrowing money from her father—and who, according to some scholars who'd visited Nancy and her brother, had modeled Bloom after Nancy's Jewish grandfather), and Brendan Behan. Behan had visited Nancy and Ralph in Spéracèdes six months before his death—they were close lifelong friends (he mentions Spéracèdes in *Confessions of an Irish Rebel*)—and his visit, during which he'd drunk his way from door to door, and had performed a mock mass in the village square, in front of the *bistro*—was legend to the villagers. When, somewhat awed by the fact of these friendships, we made some remark which indicated the extent of our wonder, she had only said, somewhat embarrassed: "Oh, Dublin's really a small place, you know—all the literary people knew one another."

During the three and a half weeks we lived with her in the summer of 1968, Betsey would get up early—at sunrise—and spend five or six hours tieing up jasmine plants with raffia. I typed away in a room above the kitchen (Ralph's paintings around me); there was not a time during July when there were less than ten people for lunch or dinner. Friends from Ireland, England, other parts of France, Switzerland, Germany (having fled Ireland in the twenties because of their revolutionary IRA politics, her family had settled in Germany—only to flee again in the thirties) were always arriving and leaving.

Memory: the look on the face of an American man who—with his wife and daughter—had rented the house next to Nancy's for the summer. They were from North Hollywood, California. His own wife had, on her first day, inquired about services—someone to watch her girl, someone to help her with cooking and cleaning (the house they rented at $600 a month was four years old), someone to pick up and deliver laundry, etc. Seeing Nancy in the fields tieing up jasmine, seeing her feed the chickens, noting (the wife with a look of anal-retentive horror) the utter chaos Nancy's kitchen was always in, they had, obviously, taken her for one of the local "peasants." We smiled with great pleasure then, when the man's jaw literally dropped at the sight of the meal which Nancy was, at lunchtime on that day, serving to thirteen people: homemade pizza (with olives and anchovies), *blanquette de veau,* homemade apple pie, wine, fruits, cheeses—he looked from the table to the kitchen, from the kitchen to the table, agape, wondering, obviously, how such food could ever have emerged from such chaos and (Nancy's own word at times) "filth." (Nancy had a wood-burning stove which she used only in winter, and a three-burner gas stove which worked at half-strength and at one speed.)

During July, Betsey designated herself Nancy's apprentice and after long lunches eaten outside under a grape-hung trellis, we'd often go to a nearby stream at St. Cassien for an afternoon swim.

Nancy was happiest, I think, during the moments when she would hear footsteps and know someone was arriving; the back door to the kitchen would swing open (it came from the *cave* where Nancy made and stored her wine—the center of the stone farmhouse, according to several *maçons* from the region who had repaired part of it, was between eight hundred and a thousand years old) and some of our friends, heads bent to avoid knocking them, would enter. Nancy's eyes would sparkle then, and more often than not she would say—"I had a thought that you would be coming by today—"

Her greatest delight—when they would leave a few hours later—would be in saying, as she did most times: "Jacques [or Bill or Jeannot or Jim] seemed in good form today, didn't he?"

Several mornings a week, as I was finishing breakfast, Bill Wiser would stop by our house and the two of us would walk to the post office together. We had come to Spéracèdes through Bill, who'd been living there for two years with his wife, Michelle (Belgian), his four-year-old son, Eric, and his daughter, Ann-Karine (who had been born in Grasse in January, 1967). Bill was "the other American writer" in Spéracèdes, and I'd been introduced to him through our literary agent, who, knowing I was going to Europe for a year, had suggested I write to him. (I did, inquiring about the area, and receiving in return letters with drawings of available houses—complete with pictures of chickens, chicken coops.) Michelle had first known the region when her family had fled there during the Nazi occupation of Belgium. Like Betsey, Michelle was a painter—she and Bill had met aboard ship when she was returning to Belgium after having spent a year in America, studying art on a Fulbright; Bill was on his way to Paris—to live, travel, write.

Bill had grown up in Georgia and Kentucky, brought up for the most part by a bachelor uncle, and he had never gone beyond high school. He'd joined the Navy at eighteen, had drifted from job to job—factories, libraries, hotels, restaurants—and had only begun writing seriously

in his late twenties (he is almost forty now)—at first publishing "filler" items in rural magazines and newspapers,
and later publishing stories and articles regularly in
places such as *Antioch Review, Kenyon Review, Playboy,
The Reporter, Cosmopolitan,* and *Carleton Miscellany.*

Having started later, his attitude toward writing was
—outwardly, at least—easier, more philosophic than mine:
he worked slowly, steadily, and saw himself hitting his
stride as a writer sometime in his late forties or early fifties. He imagined that he would by then, still be pursuing
the same daily routine. We would talk on the way to the
post office (he and Michelle teased me—as all our friends
did—about my mail obsession: I could distinguish, for example, and would stop walking when I did, the sound of
the postal truck motor from a quarter mile away); we'd
wait, cramped in the three-by-five-foot space on this side
of the counter for Georgette or her mother to give us our
mail (they sorted much of it on an ironing board); then
Bill—his lunch packed in his briefcase—would begin his
daily mile and a half walk to Cabris, the village perched
above Spéracèdes (the climb was at a steady 45-degree
angle)—where he worked in a single room which he
rented for ten dollars a month.

Most afternoons—toward five—he'd stop by on his
way home for a drink (scotch) and we'd talk again—about
the day's mail, about the replies we'd written, about the
letters (from our agent) we hadn't received, about publishers, about the day's work ("did my three pages again,"
Bill would say), about books, politics, New York, the de-
clining short-story market, the quality of typewriter rib-
bons, the French character (what Bill loved about France
was that, he often said, like himself, "it wasn't made for
the twentieth century"), our life in Spéracèdes, the future.

Betsey and Michelle would often spend mornings
and afternoons painting together, and we'd spend two or

three evenings a week with them. (In the corner of their living room-dining room was a sloping old French couch, on which each of us was obliged to lie whenever we began talking about our mothers, our families.) After dinner Bill would read Eric his bedtime story (when Michelle had returned from the hospital after he was born, Bill had gone at once to the bookcase, had taken down his Complete Shakespeare, and had begun reading to Eric from *Hamlet*), and then the four of us would sit around the fireplace and talk. What I remember most about evenings spent with them is that we seemed to always be laughing. Bill was generally shy—but when the four of us were alone he would let go: special renditions of old-time songs ("If I Give Up the Saxophone Will You Come Back to Me?"); stories of his monastic existence in cold-water flats on the Lower East Side; tales of his days as a bellhop in Miami Beach: glass of wine in one hand, he would recreate the bow he executed to guests arriving at the Seville Hotel, and would describe for us the waist-pinching toreador costume he wore.

Like Betsey and me, Jacques and Nadine were at home almost all the time—they worked together in one half of their bedroom (converted to studio)—making lampshades. Jacques traveled from village to village, finding antiques, buying them, selling them, turning them into lamps. Like Bill, he had held dozens of jobs, and like Bill, he was a born storyteller: endless tales of his days as a salesman on the island of Corsica, of the time he and Nadine (and Jeannot and Jacqueline) had been part of a mad commune run by a former concentration camp victim (who, as Jacques now analyzed it, was trying to turn every community he became part of back into the German camp of his childhood), of the years during and after the war when he had not come to terms with the fact that he was Jewish. The discovery, when he was in his late

twenties, of his Jewishness had become a central part of
his life, and we talked often of Jewish history and tradi-
tions, we made—that spring—a Passover Seder in Jacques's
house, the first one he'd ever been to.

Jacques's mother had died in Auschwitz, and he had
been brought up in the Vichy part of France during the
war. I remember him telling me one story about a German officer who had tried—for what Jacques remembered
as an entire afternoon—to get him, with bribes of money
and candy, to read to the officer from a text which, since
it was in Hebrew, Jacques had honestly found unintelligi-
ble.

As a merchant and salesman, Jacques was a master—
and he often (though less and less during our sixteen
months in Spéracèdes) related this to his Jewish origins,
telling marvelous jokes about Jewish trickery, cunning,
avarice. The great—the magical thing, he once said, was
that—even before he'd known the full truth about his
background—he had always imagined that the ideal pro-
fession for any man was the following: "You get a car and
you go into one village. There you buy some goods,
cheap, and travel to the next village where you sell the
goods at a higher price, and buy new goods. Then. . . ."
In this way, Jacques said, you could see the world, be
your own boss, earn a living, and bring happiness to people. (Jacques was often proudest that—merely by entering
the antique shops of his clients—he could make them
smile.)

Jacques and Nadine (they were in their early thirties
and had three children: Marie-Lise, Sarah, Emmanuel)
earned a good living—better every year, and the more
they earned the less they worked. This was Jacques's philosophy, secret, morality. More money meant more free
time: to read, to talk, to go horseback riding, to discover
new interests, to travel. During our time in Spéracèdes,

his work went so well that the number of days per week that he worked diminished from five to three. While we were there, he and Nadine took trips to Ireland (where they stayed with one of Nancy's friends), to Paris, to the Ardèche region of France. (The latter trip being paid for, Jacques proudly recounted when he returned, by the purchase of antiques, which, on the way home, he sold at a profit in Aix-en-Provence.)

The happier one was, Jacques maintained, the less one needed: I would, he often told me, if my life were good enough, eventually lose the need to write, the need for words . . . something which, toward the end of our stay in Spéracèdes, almost seemed to be coming true.

Eating, sleeping, visiting with friends, gardening, walking—why do any more? And often, during the last month or two of our time in Spéracèdes, we didn't. Our group had grown by then—a Canadian writer and his family (wife and four children) had, through a mutual friend, settled in a house above the village; the son of one of Nancy's friends had settled on Nancy's property (Bene was twenty-two, his wife Tania twenty; they had two children) where we all helped him—over the course of several months—build his own house; Jeannot and Jacqueline moved across the road from us with their three children and set up a silk-screening studio in their attic; we all became closer with Georgette and her husband Jo (a chef in Cannes), and often listened to her tell us of what Spéracèdes had been like twenty-five and thirty years ago, when she had been a little girl growing up there.

I had come to Spéracèdes in order, for the first time in my life, to have nothing to do for a full year except write fiction. Once in Spéracèdes, however, I found that certain events (from America) were with me continuously —unless I dealt with them directly, I felt, they would continue to haunt, they could invade my fiction in ways I would, I knew, be unable to control. Rather than try to fictionalize my political experiences—something I had no desire to do—I would come to terms with the material, would (the word I used) exorcise it by writing about it, dealing with it directly. Only when I had accomplished this would I be able to get on with what was—still, always—most important: the writing of fiction.

By the time I'd finished the bulk of the narrative, however, I found that I was feeling, for the first time in over ten years, little desire to write fiction. Jacques smiled knowingly, said nothing. I was able, for several months in the winter of 1968–69 to do no writing whatsoever and—also for the first time in my life—not to be bothered by the fact. I still rose early, I walked into town for the day's bread, I ate breakfast, I went upstairs, I read books, I wrote letters, I talked with Betsey while she painted, I did the day's shopping, I stopped in the *bistro*, I helped prepare our meals, I worked in the garden, I took long walks, I visited with friends. Our daily life seemed full enough, complete enough. My past writings were—this also for the first time—suddenly bringing in enough money for us to live on.

Like other American writers, I'd originally left the country in order to write a novel. Instead, I wrote these reflections and found myself returning to America when they were done, when I didn't have to return. I thought the reason for going back had to do, not with things political or with any events that were taking place in the U.S., but with my writing, with my desire to be a writer. Though I didn't mind the fact that I wasn't writing, I laughed at myself, at the writer still inside me who made me want to alter this fact; i.e., I still had the desire not to lose the desire to write the novel I'd originally left the country to write.

The writing I'd done in Spéracèdes—most of the narrative which follows—had dealt, in a literal way, with my life in America, with what I thought had been a specifically political journey which had begun at twenty-two, when I was a junior executive trainee for GM, and which had ended at twenty-nine, when I'd left America. I knew I would return to the writing of fiction, though, only if I went back, touched home, saw my city, and felt again those things which had previously—always—fired my desire to put words on pages.

TWO: *North from Brooklyn*

"Forward, forward," shrieked Mahmoud Ali, whose every utterance had become a yell. "Down with the Collector, down with the Superintendent of Police."

"Mr. Mahmoud Ali, this is not wise," implored the Nawab Bahadur: he knew that nothing was gained by attacking the English, who had fallen into their own pit and had better be left there; moreover, he had great possessions and deprecated anarchy.

—E. M. Forster. *A Passage to India.*

Until I was five years old I believed that the parades each year on Memorial Day were for me. I remember most the regiments of black Sea Scouts who shuffled down Linden Boulevard, around the corner from our apartment—their white hats, white belts, white boots. I grew up in a lower-middle-class section of Brooklyn (in Flatbush), and though my own block had been about half-Jewish, half-Catholic, my public school (kindergarten through eighth grade) had been 50 percent nonwhite, a fact that hadn't occurred to me until after my first novel was published. I was twenty-eight years old then, and, going through some old papers which had been left at my parents' apartment, I came across my graduation picture:

only eighteen of the thirty-five faces were white, and I was surprised, pleased—pleased that I was surprised.

Although I was told (endlessly) that the Jews were a persecuted people, an oppressed minority, in the Brooklyn of my boyhood Jews seemed to be a majority. One time some Catholic kids from around the corner (Rogers Avenue) had split open the top of my head by beating me with the buckle of a navy belt (they had caught me alone on my way home from Hebrew School), but even their steady chant, while they swung the belt—"Dirty Jew! Dirty Jew!"—seemed to me nothing more than one of the daily hazards that went with growing up in a Catholic-Jewish neighborhood.

The Jews were generally the smartest students in my school, and I was persuaded early in life that good grades led to good futures. As a boy, I had a conditioned, un-thinking pride in successful Jews, especially in Jewish athletes (wasn't it true that Hank Greenberg could have broken Babe Ruth's home-run record if only he'd played on *Yom Kippur?*) In our neighborhood, when our num-bers were equal to theirs (as they usually were), most fights with Catholics remained verbal, and when they didn't, we were able to hold our own.

If anything, being Jewish in my section of Brooklyn in the years following the Second World War not only made me feel special, but, inevitably, superior. Thus, when my parents let me know that they had not pressed charges against the boys who'd split open the top of my head (that night, when I'd become weak and dizzy, my parents whispered about "brain damage"; I awoke in the morning with—an accident?—the *German* measles), they impressed upon me the conditions of the boys' homes. My mother had visited the house of each of the boys who'd attacked me. As in my home, the mothers of all the Cath-olic boys worked—but here similarities ended: most important, as my mother described the findings of her visits, the homes these boys lived in were "not-well-taken-care-of." In some there were no fathers, in others the fathers "drank-a-lot." Result: the children were truants, they did poorly in school. They were our poor-whites, and, my parents felt, not to blame for what they had done to me. They did not come from good Jewish homes; they were "less fortunate" than I was.

I suppose there were right-wingers in my Brooklyn neighborhood (Catholic boys I went to school with sold the *Brooklyn Tablet* outside Holy Cross Church on Sundays, a paper I later discovered was notorious for its anti-semitism and its support of Father Coughlin), but I don't remember them. All my relatives, all my parents' friends read *The New York Post* or *The New York Times*. America was, as far as I could tell, a free country, a place in which, if he worked hard, as I was forever taught, a Jew could become a success.

All men seemed to be judged—as guys were in the schoolyard—by their abilities. The best athlete in my school was a friend of mine, and black. He received the school Citizenship Award when we graduated. Other classmates, also black, waited with me to take our younger brothers and sisters home from the same nursery school. My friend Benny from around the corner (his father was the superintendent of an apartment house) was black and he came to my house and I went to his. As for the world which existed beyond my block, beyond my school, hadn't my beloved Brooklyn Dodgers (I was born several blocks from Ebbets Field) dealt the deathblow to all discrimination in America by bringing Jackie Robinson into the major leagues?

That almost all the black children in my public school lived in one neighborhood—in what seemed to me at the time a rather pleasant section of wood-frame houses—was no more unusual than the fact that most of the Jews lived in my neighborhood. That some of the black boys and girls had to go to work at a younger age than I did was only a fact which made their lives seem slightly more exciting, adventurous. I was, myself, proud that I began working after school before most of my friends did.

That all cleaning women and janitors were black was something neither I—nor anybody around me—ever questioned. It was only when I was in college that my brother and I began—like some older cousins—referring to the woman who cleaned for our mother as "the family slave." The woman worked only for my mother's family—and there were telephone calls weekly in which my mother and her four sisters would "trade her around"—"You take the girl this Thursday and I'll give her back to you next week." My family could only afford to have her once every two weeks. The successful sister had her several times a week.

It was not, in fact, the blacks who were feared in my school and neighborhood. This status was enjoyed by the Italians. To gain immunity (body and property) one had to be friends with a member of one of their gangs. During my last two years of grade school one of my friends was —his real name—Victor Paradise; Vic's older brother was chief of a gang named "The Tigers," famous for legendary Prospect Park zip-gun and switchblade battles. Vic's girl-friend and mine, both Jewish, were friends, and we went to parties together on weekends, played ball together afternoons; he called me Robert Taylor and I called him Farley Granger.

I did not grow up in a Marxist-Leninist-Socialist-Jewish home (the man who killed Trotsky, I'm now told, was a distant cousin of my grandmother): in fact, one of my few childhood political memories concerns a distant uncle, whom we visited rarely; the visits were dangerous excursions as I remember them, steeped in mystery. My uncle's small apartment, in a distant section of Brooklyn, was dusty, filled with books and huge brown-edged posters of men with beards. My uncle was a tall man and looked, everyone agreed, exactly like Abraham Lincoln; when I knew him he was sick and lay always in a large four-poster bed, his eyes set in deep hollows above marvelous protruding cheekbones. Sometimes he would rise to his elbows and argue passionately, eyes glowing.

Each time we left his home my father would say the same thing: he respected Uncle Ben for believing in something (I don't think he ever used the word "communism" in my presence) and devoting his life to it—but would Uncle Ben have been allowed to hold similar opinions against the Russian government if he lived there?

The answer was obvious, the argument irrefutable. Everything around me—parents, school, books, radio programs—supported the proposition that "only in America" could a man like my mysterious uncle not be put in prison.

Sports, at least until the age of fourteen, were my whole life. When my father came home from work each night, I'd kiss him, grab *The New York Post* from under his arm, and run to my room. Afterwards, if he saw me reading it, he'd ask—angrily—why I always read the back pages—the sports section—before the front pages. When I graduated from public school, in my autograph book I listed two possibilities under "Career Ambition": professional baseball player, commercial artist. At five-foot-four or -five and 115 pounds I had a huge rainbow curve which I would aim at the batter's shoulder or ear, and which I would then watch break across the outside corner of the plate. It kept me ahead of the batters, drew incredulous spectators to the rear of backstops. It also enabled me—by proudly telling everyone that it was my father who had taught me how to throw my curve and my "sinker"—to try to reach him, to draw him back into the magic of that world we'd existed in together that first evening in our backyard (garages, not grass) when he had taught me my most treasured skill. I was ten or eleven and we were having a catch together when one of the balls he threw to me curved—I gaped, and asked him how he did it; he showed me, and the first time I held the ball in the new position, and turned my wrist at the last moment of delivery, the ball had spun off my fingers, and as it made its way across what must have been the forty or fifty feet between us, it dipped beautifully down and away.

My father, raised in an extremely Orthodox Jewish family, wanted his sons to be "Americans": my mother had named me Jacob Mordecai (for my father's father), but three days after I was born, my father changed the name to an "American" one—Jay Michael. And though my mother, who had not been brought up in an Orthodox manner, had enrolled me in the Crown Heights Yeshiva (hoping to please my father and his family, I imagine), my father had fought her on the issue, and, after a few brief months, had succeeded in having me transferred to P. S. 246. I helped his cause immensely, as I remember it, by screaming and crying my heart out on Columbus Day (or was it Christmas?)—when all my friends from the block had a holiday and I had to ride the Nostrand Avenue bus, schoolbooks hidden under my coat, to Yeshiva. "I'm an American! I'm an American!" I kept yelling.

Like all their friends and relatives, my parents worshiped Roosevelt. During newsreels at the Granada Theater on Church Avenue, everybody would applaud when his face appeared on the screen. One afternoon in 1944 some friends and I stationed ourselves beneath a window in my backyard, and when my landlord's daughter appeared, we sprang up and shouted in singsong the ultimate taunt: "Vera votes for Dew-ey! Vera votes for Dew-ey!"

I went to high school during the McCarthy era, but I did not remember that my father had warned me against signing petitions until, during an argument years later (thinking I had held it against him), he reminded me that he had done so. I do remember that some of my teachers would preface discussions with the statement: "Now don't go home and tell your parents I'm a Communist, but . . ." After school I don't recall mentioning such things. Nor do I recall a single discussion among friends which was even vaguely political.

I worked all through high school, beginning with a job at five dollars a week plus tips in a dry-cleaning store when I was thirteen years old and a high school freshman. The owner, Mr. Berman, gave me a discount on any of my own clothes I had cleaned—and a 20 percent commission on business (from friends and family) I brought in. I spent a lot of my time riding buses to sections of Brooklyn where he had owned other tailor shops, trying to collect unpaid bills for him. Mr. Berman left me in charge of the store often and this pleased me. The first evening he did this I found a dollar on the floor in the back room, under a rack of clothes. I gave the dollar to him when he returned; he put his arm around my shoulder (I was taller than he was) and told me that he had left the bill there purposely, as a test which I had just passed. When I told my parents the story I couldn't understand why they became angry.

At various times I worked as an elevator operator, mail-order clerk, waiter, busboy, tutor, postal worker, delivery boy. Almost all the jobs had a sense of adventure attached to them—I was a yeoman on a merchant marine ship one summer, I trucked racks of clothes in and out of cars along Eighth Avenue, I rode the subways into new sections of the city to deliver packages.

The work was the means to an end—and the end was always in sight. During high school I worked for pocket money, for college; during college I worked for my education; during the summers I worked to pay for the coming school year. . . . All jobs were temporary.

Someday, I knew, I would get what was spoken of in my home in magical tones—a college education. An education, I'd been told ever since I could remember, was "something nobody could ever take away from you." To lower-middle-class Jewish families such as mine, living still with the irrational and profound fear that anything you owned could be snatched away in a moment (my grandmother had been smuggled across the Russian border during a pogrom; a friend of the family, the legend went, had once, during a pogrom, watched her eldest son dig his own grave), nonmaterial possessions were the most valuable ones.

I enrolled in Columbia College in the fall of 1955, and during my four years there I cannot remember seeing, even once, a political demonstration or a petition. At Columbia in the late fifties we prided ourselves on our apolitical sophistication, our "disinterestedness." The largest turnout for any election held during my years there came during my senior year, when we proudly voted to abolish all student government.

The members of the college administration, like ourselves, were enlightened men. If there were injustices, grievances, problems, inequities—administrative doors were open to us, things could be discussed rationally, solutions arrived at in a civilized manner. Nobody thought about questioning the following regulation from the college catalog concerning "Academic Discipline":

The continuance of each student upon the rolls of the College, the receipt by him of academic credits, his graduation, and the conferring of the degree are strictly subject to the disciplinary powers of the University, which is free to cancel his registration at any time on any grounds which it deems advisable. The disciplinary authority of the University is vested in the President, in such cases as he deems proper, and, subject to the reserved powers of the President, in the Dean of the College.

In those years (the Silent Eisenhower years, as they would be called in the sixties) we must have supported Martin Luther King's bus boycott—but I don't remember doing so. Birmingham was far away. Harlem was equally far—on the *other* side of Morningside Park; and we all laughed during Freshman Orientation Week when an upperclassman warned us about not taking the "wrong" subway line to that "other" 116th Street stop.

If more recent Columbia undergraduates have carried Fanon, Malcolm, Ché, and Marcuse under their arms, we stuck to Yeats, Freud, Faulkner, and Tolstoy. Our fiercest opinions had to do with ideas and literature. Our heroes were our professors, and we looked up to them, we respected them; we did not think of ourselves as being against them. We were cynical about any political action, and we admired our professors for their articulate cynicism, for their own disinterested attitude toward the world, for their ability to cut down students and other professors with witty remarks. "Well," the teacher I had for my first advanced writing course would say after reading a student's story to us, "it seems to me there's less here than meets the eye."

Between classes, after classes, we would sit along the wall in front of Hamilton Hall, or on Broadway, in Riker's (the fraternity set could afford to sit in Prexy's, which served "the hamburger with a college education"; I ate there once and forever after envied—and resented—those who did not have to think about the amount of money they spent for lunch), and talk about our courses, our teachers, the papers we were writing, the latest remarks, gossip.

Like my friends, I was proud of how much reading and writing the College required; during my four years at Columbia I must have averaged at least ten to fifteen pages of writing per week. All through Freshman Orientation Week, I remember, we reveled in legends of the prodigious amounts of work required by Columbia's Contemporary Civilization and Humanities courses: our first assignment, we proudly told one another, and—after—friends from other colleges, was to read—overnight—the entire *Iliad*.

I remember how impressed I was one night during Freshman Week when a sophomore explained the high point of his freshman year to us: the praise he'd received from his Humanities professor—a famous literary critic—for having been the only student to understand the true magic of *Don Quixote*. "What I wrote," the sophomore explained to us (we were sitting on the lush leather-covered chairs of Hartley Hall Lounge), "was that the Don was really the only sane man in a mad world: thus, you see, the windmills *are* giants. . . ." Illusion, he explained, because powered by a superior imagination, was more real than reality. His reversing of a traditional view seemed, at the time, the most staggering—and admirable —of accomplishments.

That spring, near the end of my second semester, I sat up in bed almost until dawn one night, to give my brother Robert, who was just finishing junior high school, an elaborate *explication de texte* of the first few pages of Camus's *L'Étranger*. Robert, who at thirteen listed "Poet" as his career ambition, sat on his side of our hi-riser as I whispered, in a style of criticism which I was thrilled to possess, to be able to share, about endless nuances of language and significance.

During our years at Columbia, we learned, we were going to become "whole men" (the "w" dropped from the phrase when we referred, knowingly, to our sister school Barnard, across Broadway). We were going to become familiar with the major literature, art, music, and history of Western Civilization—and we were going to do so in small intimate classes which would be taught (even at an introductory level) by some of the world's most distinguished scholars. (Men such as Mark Van Doren, Moses Hadas, Douglas Moore, Donald Frame, and Lionel Trilling.)

Any questioning we did was, literally, academic: was James Shenton (donning a raccoon coat and having Barnard girls dress as flappers during his lecture on the Roaring Twenties) merely a sensationalist? Was Mark Van Doren's gentle angelic eloquence a subtle form of sentimentality? Why was Lionel Trilling so esteemed by the world when, as a classroom teacher, he seemed barely the equal—in range, in articulateness—of men such as Andrew Chiappe and F. W. Dupee?

A man such as C. Wright Mills, who taught at Columbia when I was there, was a hero to us, not for his political radicalism, but for his uniqueness as a teacher, as an individual. (He rode to Columbia on a motorcycle, he'd married his Puerto Rican secretary.) We were proud to have a brilliant maverick among us.

We collected no data on Columbia's involvement in the military-industrial complex, on its role as a slumlord; instead we savored gossip, legends concerning teachers, former students (many, in those years, about Ginsberg and Kerouac), and clever remarks—e.g., Irwin Edman,

NORTH FROM BROOKLYN 65

some years before, stopping a Faculty Club discourse on President (of Columbia) Eisenhower, by observing that "the trouble with the General, gentlemen, is that he has delusions of adequacy."

I had not, before I entered Columbia, ever considered becoming a writer. Not, at least, since the time when, at nine years old, I'd written a novel: I'd been in the fourth grade then, and for about two months I wrote one chapter a week—which my mother dutifully typed for me—and each Monday morning I would stand in front of my class and read the new chapter to them. By the time I stopped, the novel was between thirty and forty pages long, the chapters two to four pages each, typed—thanks to an old typewriter—in glorious half-red and half-black lettering.

At the start of my first year at Columbia I listed as my probable professional choices, Advertising, Television Producing and Directing, and Architectural Engineering. Once a week, regularly, I would meet with my advisor, the late Andrew Chiappe (whose Shakespeare course was already legend in the college—the best course I ever had), and do my best to engage him in the discussion of "what I wanted to be."

By the end of the first year—due in part to my courses and teachers (in particular, to a freshman composition course I took with Charles Van Doren), and in part to the antimaterialist ethic which pervaded the Columbia cultural scene—I decided to become an English major. By the end of my sophomore year, having glutted my program with writing and literature courses, I began (with announcements to all teachers and friends) my first novel. I began it, in fact, within two weeks of my operation—so that it would be finished before I died a year later. I shared the novel with Robert—reading each chapter to him when it was done. I finished the novel during the summer between my sophomore and junior years, and the following fall, I showed it to Charles Van Doren who became excited about it and sent it to several publishers on my behalf.

I remember one time, in the fall of my junior year, after I'd shown him the rejection letter I'd received from a publisher, trying to shrug it off. It didn't really bother me, I said. We were walking down the steps that led from Low Library to College Walk, and he laughed: "Come on," he said. "It bothers you. It's as if somebody had told you your child was ugly." I shrugged again, admitted he was right, and smiled. I repeated his remark to everyone—and I continued to submit the novel, to write, to enjoy the status of being—at nineteen—that most romantic of types: an unpublished novelist.

For my first three years of college I lived at home, sharing a nine-by-twelve-foot bedroom with Robert, traveling two hours a day on the IRT with my books and lunchbag. I never began writing until everyone else at home was asleep. Then I would move into the kitchen, push the dishes and oilcloth aside in order to have the smooth maple surface of the table to press pen and pencil against, and stay up until two or three in the morning working on my novels, essays, stories. My typewriter—an ancient heavy Royal—would rest, to muffle its sounds, on towels. The weak light from the overhead fixture always seemed stronger when the rest of the house was dark and quiet—and there was something tangible about the empty surfaces of the yellow enameled walls (the only ones in the house not overloaded with pictures and knickknacks).

My quiet was disturbed once a night, ritually, when my father, sometime between one and two in the morning would get up to go to the bathroom. He would peer into the kitchen rather blearily (he could not see too well, having gone blind in one eye in his thirties), and, shielding his eyes against the light, his head tilted to one side in order to focus better with his good eye, he would say to me irritably, in Yiddish: "From this you're going to earn a living?"

He would shake his head despairingly, scornfully—and I would think silent angry thoughts: what had *he* ever accomplished in life to allow him to talk to me about earning a living? A second later I would hear the splashing of his urine in the toilet, and when he went by me again, I would hear the sounds of his disapproval clucking liquidly in his mouth. His pajamas always sagged; they were too big for his small frame.

The central fact of my life during my years at Columbia—as it had been since childhood—was the tension that resulted in my home from the fact that my mother was forced to work. Again and again during those nights in the kitchen I would turn the self-pity I was feeling for myself into rage—and generally the rage was directed against my father. Never, as I recall it, against anything as abstract as Society or The System.

My father's business consisted of the rental of a desk in a printing company's office, from where he tried to develop, as a "jobber," a trade of his own. He was a stubborn and intelligent man who did not, during those years, want to work for anyone but himself. During my high school years I always looked forward to Christmas and Easter vacations because I would spend most of my time in "the city" with my father—sitting in his office, talking with him, visiting his clients (he was obviously proud of me, proud to introduce me as his *kaddishal*), delivering packages for him.

The first thing we would do every time would be to visit the printing plant: the presses were loud and huge, and my father would always introduce me to the printers, would show me a printing job of his own which was in process.

In addition to the tour of the printing plant, I would get to do, every day, something our family did only a few times a year—eat in a restaurant. Invariably, I would order scrambled eggs, french fries, toast and jelly—always amazed that I could get such a full plate for such a low price (thirty-five or forty cents), always impressed by the size of the tip my father would leave, by the easy way in which he'd kibbitz with the waitresses. Like the receptionists who took packages of printing from me, the waitresses obviously liked my father, and this pleased me.

I also liked the grown-up feeling that came with the fact that my father would confide financial secrets to me: despite what my mother said, he'd usually hint, things were going well—orders were coming in—he would soon be able to repay his debts and be out from under. Somehow, though, he never did get out from under the debts, and—what pained him most in life—this meant that my mother had to continue to work.

She worked as a Registered Nurse, and sometimes as an administrator of fund-raising campaigns for the Muscular Dystrophy charities. As often as she changed the furniture in our tiny four-room Brooklyn apartment (so that it would seem new, larger, different), she would change the shifts she worked at the hospital (8 to 4, 4 to 12, 12 to 8), and she often worked double shifts, took double cases. My father's sole end in life, it often seemed to me as a boy, was the assumption of my mother's household duties (washing clothes, cleaning the apartment, doing the dishes). Though I have pleasant memories of the conversations I had with him when I helped him at work, at home his longest conversations with me were the short-tempered sentences he'd spit out when my actions—

usually by omission—showed ingratitude, lack of consideration for my mother.

Afternoons and evenings when, because of the night shift my mother was recuperating from, our house moved on tiptoes and any minor sound (the telephone, like my typewriter, rested on towels) brought my father's hand into the air to strike me or Robert—I sometimes felt a hatred for him that overwhelmed me.

During my senior year at Columbia—with the help of a gift from my parents—I moved out of my home in Brooklyn and lived with a friend, Arnie Offner, in a furnished apartment on West 107th Street. Our bachelor life was more than I'd hoped for: we each had girlfriends; I cooked for myself (making cheeseburgers out of chopped meat I bought from a local butcher at nineteen cents a pound, and *Velveeta*); I worked furiously on a new novel; I lived in as much dirt as I pleased; I became closer with Robert, who would visit often, and sleep over. Away from home, we talked endlessly about books, girls, school, writing—and home.

Under the guidance of Richard Chase, I completed my second novel by the end of the year. "*I* don't see any reason why it shouldn't be published," he wrote to me that summer, and offered to write a letter for me to his own publisher. The following fall, like the majority of my friends, I found myself—mainly for lack of knowing what else to do—in graduate school: on a fellowship to Indiana University, a school with which Columbia faculty—Chase, Steven Marcus, Lionel Trilling—had been associated. I had, I thought, two purposes in going there: to get farther away from Brooklyn, and to support myself while I began a third novel.

THREE: *My Blessing Not My Doom*

> For the man in the paddock, whose duty it is to sweep up manure, the supreme terror is the possibility of a world without horses. To tell him that it is disgusting to spend one's life shoveling up hot turds is a piece of imbecility. A man can get to love shit if his livelihood depends on it . . .
>
> —Henry Miller. *Tropic of Cancer.*

I dropped out of graduate school the following spring (1960) and took a position with the General Motors Corporation as a Junior Executive Trainee. At the time, General Motors had been looking for a liberal arts graduate to be part of a special one-year training program, in order to see what would happen to someone with no preconceptions, no education in engineering and/or business administration. They wanted, they insisted, a "fresh, honest viewpoint."

I wanted to write novels. It was, still, the only thing that mattered to me: by not attending classes at Indiana University, I'd completed my third unpublished novel, and I wanted to begin a fourth. The Dean of the Graduate School had already called me into his office to tell me that he didn't think Indiana University was the place to do it (I agreed), and so, the biographies of other American novelists strong in my imagination, I'd been looking, on and off for six months, for a job that would be just that: a job—separate in all ways from my writing, a means to an end only, something that would give me the time, money, and freedom of mind to write. I would work during the day and write at night, and there would be none of the inner conflicts that had plagued me during my nine months in graduate school—i.e., between being a critic of literature, and a writer of the literature others criticized.

Two weeks after my twenty-second birthday—on June 16, 1960—I went to work at Chevrolet-Indianapolis, a body-stamping plant employing about three thousand blue-collar and five hundred white-collar workers. There were four others in the training program—two engineers and two business administration graduates. Our salaries were excellent, fringe benefits generous, and for the first year we were not supposed to do any real work; we would observe only—spending about half our time in the factory, half in the executive offices. Once a month we would submit reports, and at the end of the year we would be appointed to our first executive positions.

The five of us started in different departments, changed assignments weekly, and were, in this way, to learn, by the end of the year, how all the departments and divisions and subdivisions of one automotive plant were interrelated, linked, organized. Moreover, in order to know exactly what was involved in the various jobs over which we might someday hold responsibility we worked in the factory with the union men—loading boxcars, shoveling coal, welding parts, working on assembly lines. In truth, as good as the prospects seemed for someone wanting to get ahead as a junior executive, they

3

seemed even better for someone wanting to write novels.

I was hopeful, optimistic. Working in a factory was, I felt, infinitely more "real" than being a graduate student, and though I—and friends—found it amusing that I should suddenly be an Organization Man, I can't recall that I felt at all uncomfortable about taking the position. My girlfriend, Ginny, and my closest friend, Arnie Offner —he too was a graduate student at Indiana—gave me presents to mark the occasion. From my girlfriend, bermuda shorts and a sport shirt "For the Conservative Executive" —and from Arnie, a Parker Pen, and a card which said: "Someday I want you to autograph a book for me: Good luck at GM, executive."

I had no particular interest in General Motors, cars, engineering, or business administration, but I didn't see anything particularly wrong in them. Certainly I had no objections that were in any way political. As an executive, I might, I even told myself, be able to do some good someday. What kind of good I didn't know—but I assumed that anyone who possessed power in the largest corporation in America would also possess the power to affect the lives of many men.

I spent my first week at GM reading stacks of company literature: the role of Chevrolet in the General Motors Corporation, the role of our plant in the Chevrolet Division, the role of the spot-welder in the door-assembly line, etc. Two other trainees and I were left in a pleasant air-conditioned room, told to relax, to read, and to ask questions when we had any—the Assistant Director of Personnel, Ralph Sharpe, had an office across from us. On my first day Ralph had taken me on a tour of the plant and offices, had taken me to lunch in the executive cafeteria, had introduced me to all the department heads, had told me about all the plans—stock option, car purchase, pension, health insurance, life insurance, disability—that awaited me in my new life.

I remember only two things that I read that week: the first was the story—told as if part of an adventure novel—of how the man who had founded Chevrolet (Louis Chevrolet) had selected the emblem for the car from a design he noticed on the wallpaper of his hotel room one night in the early years of the century when he lay sleepless in Paris. The other was a handbook used as part of an in-service training program for foremen on how to get along well with workers. It contained personality charts which described and defined the "twelve basic human motivations"; if you ranked a worker in each category and then, via a series of arithmetical maneuvers and references to the data in a Human Motivational Chart, constructed a graph of his personality, you would be fully equipped to handle him. (There were "tried and true" methods of handling every personality "type.") There were some commonsense remarks about human nature and "interpersonal relationships," and there were case studies—examples—illustrating specific situations, problems. The one I recall: when something went wrong in your section and you knew whose fault it was, you were to approach the worker and ask him what the reason for the trouble was. "Listen politely to his answer," the handbook advised. "Then ask him for the *real* reason."

I laughed, then showed the item to the other trainees, to Ralph—I mentioned it to others; but nobody seemed to find anything unusual in the advice. Everyone took it seriously, matter-of-factly; it seemed sensible, unnoteworthy.

At the start of my second week I was assigned to the Materials-Handling Department; on my third day there I

was introduced to a middle-aged man named Henry
Jones. Jones, in charge of one of the subdivisions of the
department, put me at a desk directly behind his own,
gave me several stacks of oaktag sheets, and told me to
total—on my electric adding machine—columns of figures
from one set of sheets, and to post the totals on other
sheets.

The function of the Materials-Handling Department
was to order and keep records on all material that came
into and went out of the plant—steel, coal, wood, maintenance equipment, paint, automobile parts, office supplies,
etc. Information was accumulated ("posted") on thousands of cards, so that at any moment any individual item
—a box of pencils or a right-rear-inner-door-bracket-con-
necting-hinge, could be located.

I'd been warned (and had already discovered) that
there was, especially among the men such as Henry
Jones—middle-aged, noncollege-educated personnel who'd
spent the better part of their lives working themselves up
to their positions of minor authority—resentment of "college kids" like myself. At Chevrolet-Indianapolis many
men like Jones had begun as hourly workers in the factory; the salaries that it had taken them twenty or twenty-five years to work their way to were being reached
(and passed) in less than five by those of us with degrees.
I was, then, wary—reluctant to bother Henry, to question
anything besides the mechanical details of operations assigned to me.

For a few hours I tapped at my adding machine,
watched it gyrate and slide, and I posted the totals.
When I'd finished the first stack of cards, though, I got
up, waited at the side of Henry's desk until my presence
was acknowledged, and then asked if he could tell me
what all the numbers that crisscrossed my sheets represented.

"Just do your work, son," he said without looking up. His sleeves were rolled up, his eyes were dashing madly across order forms from behind rimless glasses. I went back to my desk and, while I watched the back of his head bob in and out to the rhythms of his work, and as he telephoned frantically to people in and out of the factory concerning materials which were either late or lost, I continued to make, at my adding machine, hundreds of thousands of calculations. I added figures from one column, pushed the total button, listened to the pleasant whirring of the machine, posted the results on other sheets. To amuse myself I invented complicated problems in multiplication and division, in order—for several seconds—to watch the machine move by itself.

The office itself was a long glass-enclosed rectangle in the North Wing of the executive building. There were three rows of desks in it (Henry had the middle row), about ten desks in each row. The supervisor of each of the three subdivisions sat at the head of each row; the clerks, young executives (trainees), and secretaries were in line at the desks behind. Except for the secretaries, each worker had an adding machine at his desk; the young executives had telephones. The desks were gray, chrome-rimmed. At the rear of the room was the desk of the Superintendent of the Material-Handling Department's secretary, and beyond this desk was his office, also glass-enclosed.

During the morning, and after lunch, I tried again to get from Henry—and that having failed, from workers who manned the desks behind my own—some explanation of what I was doing. I took my posting cards from desk to desk but nobody seemed to know the meaning of my numbers. I went back to my desk and worked until quitting time.

The man whose job I'd taken returned a day or two

later and I resisted the impulse to ask him about the numbers. I could tell the story in Bloomington on weekends, where, in the retelling its mundane insanity took on exotic qualities: I had actually lived out a paradigm of the modern condition—for one eight-hour workday, sixty minutes an hour, I had performed thousands of operations, posted thousands of figures, and had never known what any of it had meant.

For the rest of my time in the Materials-Handling Department I was usually assigned to work with one of the clerks (noncollege-graduates) or young trainees, helping them post their figures, make their calculations. When I mentioned my Henry Jones day to the others, they laughed, made some joke to the effect that Henry thought he was "going to own the company" some day (he never took coffee breaks); but none of the clerks or trainees were disturbed that they knew nothing concerning the motions I'd been through. "I don't want to know any more than I'm supposed to," was the standard line. People who wanted to know about things that went beyond their own desks were either crazy ("Where's it get you—?"), or to be distrusted ("He must be after somebody's job."). In the lower echelons of the salaried division of the corporation (the same thing proved generally true in the hourly division), brownnosing, industry, and enthusiasm were as scorned, were considered as dangerous as Henry's futile dedication.

My position was different. I was, as the Personnel Director had put it, to "get the lay of the land." I was to know what was forbidden to all others, even Henry Jones: i.e., I was to know, within a year, how—in Chevrolet-Indianapolis and similar plants—jobs, departments, men, functions, budgets, materials, and decisions were interrelated. The workers and executives under me, it followed, would then have faith in my actions and decisions because they would be able to assure themselves of what was indisputably true—that I had access to information they didn't have.

From the offices of the Materials-Handling Department I was sent to the factory, where I trucked parts, walked floors with the foremen, filled out forms in the factory office, and loaded boxcars. I don't remember which department I went to after Materials-Handling, but I do remember that the time I spent in the factory working a six-thirty to three o'clock shift always went by more quickly than the time spent in the offices. By my second or third day in the Materials-Handling offices I had become a professional clock watcher—inventing time games, dividing hours into minutes, counting seconds in my head to test my brain's accuracy against that of the world, measuring minutes to lunch hour, to coffee breaks, going to the bathroom every hour on the hour.

The days I spent at Chevrolet-Indianapolis were the longest of my life; this is what I remember above all else when I think of the months I spent there—the heaviness, the surreal slowness of time—and then, what seems, still, anything but surreal: the solidity of the factory itself—the substantiality of the concrete and steel structures, the size of the open "bays," the weight of body-stamping presses, the power of the scrap-baler, the texture, color of boxcars, overhead cranes, oil-slicked steel rolls, conveyor belts, forklift trucks, pressed-out truck sides, blackened floors, toilets, noises, girders.

The single picture that stays with me most vividly, replacing all others: four men wearing oversized safety mittens, one at each corner of a mammoth three-storey-high body-stamping press, touching two buttons twenty or twenty-five times an hour, eight hours a day, five days a week, making the press move, the die fall.

During my first few months at GM I lived by myself in a large wood-frame house on the northeast side of Indianapolis. The house belonged to Ralph's mother, and he offered it to me in order to help me out (he charged me forty dollars a month), and, at the same time, to have somebody living in the house while his mother was away in Michigan, staying with an invalid sister. Although I would sometimes sit in the downstairs living room at night, reading, I spent most of my time in the four-room apartment that constituted the upstairs part of the house. I had my own kitchen and bathroom, and I immediately turned the living room into my writing room, setting my typewriter and paper on a desk by the front window, stacking my books around me, sending my new address to the publisher then considering my novel.

Two or three weeks after I moved there, Ralph asked if I minded letting one of the other new trainees share the apartment with me for a week. Only when I saw how gladly I welcomed the offer did I notice how isolated I was already feeling. The other trainee—he was married and had two children—was pleasant and easygoing, and we got along well, shopping together for supper, playing basketball in a local schoolyard after work. Every evening, after dinner, he would help with the dishes, then say "See ya—" and head downstairs, where he would sit, watching television until one or two in the morning. He "really admired" me, he said on the way to work one morning, for all the books I had.

He went home to his family for the weekend, and I went to Bloomington to see Ginny. By the second weekend after I'd begun work, I remember telling her that something was wrong, that I knew I'd made a mistake. How could anyone, especially someone our age, someone who'd been chosen for the same job I'd been chosen for, watch five and six hours of TV five nights a week? How could grown men sit at desks, stand at presses, performing the same operations day after day? The job, the people, the house, the neighborhood—none of them were for me.

But what else could I do? This is the way most Americans lived, I said (a "discovery" I dwelt on with morbid passion), and, like them, I too was trapped: I dreaded returning to graduate school, I could conceive of no alternatives beyond those of being a student or taking a job (and all jobs, I was sure, were the same), I was doing no writing and felt that I would do none, I had nothing accepted for publication, I had no money saved, and I owed the Business Men's Clearing House of Indianapolis, the employment agency which had sent me to GM, 75 percent of my first month's salary, a debt I was paying off in monthly installments. In their office, a fifty-dollar bill had been scotchtaped to the pillar next to the desk of the man who interviewed me; the agent who placed the most people each week got the fifty dollars.

I tried to become friendly with my neighbors, and they were pleasant enough. They seemed, however, to have only one topic of conversation: *the niggers were moving in.* Sometimes, in the evenings, the little boy who lived next door would come and sit on my porch and we'd talk. In September, he would tell me that he didn't like kindergarten because his class was "full of them niggers." I showed no surprise and made a few comments designed to subvert his feelings, but he remained adamant in his hatred. The reason he hated nigger-children was simple—and he ran down from the porch, turned, and shouted it at me when I'd asked him why: "Because they're *black!*"

Each day that I worked, returned home, ate, tried to write and couldn't, I became more depressed. Away from the factory, insignificant things began to have the power to destroy me. One night—a few weeks after the other trainee had moved out—I decided to treat myself to something unusual. I took a walk to the supermarket and looked through the section of special foods, finally selecting an authentic imported Mexican dinner. After dinner, I told myself, having broken the routine of my meals, I would be able to get right to work.

The Mexican dinner was authentic—I burned the inside of my mouth almost raw on the first few bites, struggled through a few more, and then gave up and dumped the rest in the garbage. Why wouldn't anything work out right anymore? I screamed to myself. I was furious, overwhelmed by anger—and then, suddenly, I felt weak, alone, and—I couldn't believe it—there were tears dribbling down my cheeks: the dinner proved what I already believed—I had failed, I was failing, I would continue to fail; what I'd written would never be accepted for publication, and, the corollary: I would never write again.

Another evening at about the same time, unable to write, I walked to a bowling alley which was eight or nine blocks away in order to pass the time until sleep. I was confronted at the desk with a sign I'd never seen before: WE RESERVE THE RIGHT TO REFUSE SERVICE TO ANYONE. I asked the woman at the desk what the sign meant. "Just what it says, son," she replied. She was an elderly woman, her silvered hair pressed tightly to her skull in tiny curls. "You mean you refuse the right to serve Negroes, don't you?" I said.

She looked at me, stopped chewing her gum, then shrugged, gave a quick high-pitched laugh, and went back to her newspaper, her gum chewing. I turned and left, and as I walked the dark streets back to my house I felt that someone was following me. I ran the last few blocks.

I began to live only for the weekends, for the time I spent with Ginny. She would cook for me, we would go for long drives together, sleep late, talk endlessly—she tried to keep me from becoming too discouraged by the fact that I wasn't writing ("You'll be published," she kept telling me. "You'll be published. Don't worry."). I could get outside myself and my self-pity somewhat on weekends, telling GM stories and joking about my nascent political consciousness (Read all about it: YOUNG NOVELIST DISCOVERS RACISM IN MIDWEST . . . Extra! Extra! ASSEMBLY LINES DO EXIST STATES NOVELIST NEUGEBOREN . . .), but what objectivity I gained was buried on Monday morning.

I hated the factory deeply—but what, I would ask, had anyone ever promised me? What had I ever expected? The fault lay as much in me, in my expectations, as it did in the job.

My symptoms were manifold: some time during the first or second week I noticed that I felt vaguely sick to my stomach every day—the sickness beginning in the morning and ending only when I would wash up to leave work. By the end of the second month, from the time I woke until I reached the plant, I would also live with the fear that it was going to be *that* day on which I would do something marvelously antic at the factory (organize all the union men to wear white shirts and ties, give copies of *Das Kapital* to the Plant Manager and all Department Heads, invite all the Negro janitors to eat with me in the executive dining room.)

When I left the plant it was with a sublime sense of relief: eight hours had actually passed. I was always surprised. By the middle of the second month, my depression was deep and continuous: what I couldn't understand was how others, whom I assumed were not so different from myself, could push themselves through a lifetime of eight-hour days like the few I'd already pushed myself through. I projected each eight-hour day ten and twenty and thirty years ahead—by which time, I felt, my outer and inner selves would surely be equal to one another. When I looked around each day at the workers pressing their buttons and tightening their bolts (would I ever have the courage to suggest that the Personnel Department give a showing of *Modern Times* for all union men?), I had to conclude that they could perform their daily tasks only if—and this went against all the feelings that I thought had driven my desire to write novels—their external and internal worlds were equal; only if, that is, they had no inner lives.

My memories of these days at Chevrolet-Indianapolis are not all unpleasant. I enjoyed doing physical work—shoveling coal, loading boxcars, trucking tubs of parts from one section of the factory to another; and I enjoyed even more the times I would be assigned as a helper to an individual worker. It gave me a chance to talk, to get to know somebody, and to thereby regain the belief that each of the several thousand men around me was, in fact, a particular human being. I remember the pleasant feeling of my body resting against the inside of an empty coal car, relaxing under an August sun outside the factory, sweat dripping down my face, my neck, my arms, my back. The worker I was with was a husky black of twenty or twenty-one years old, handsome, with large thick lips, a bullethead, steady open eyes. During the day he shoveled coal and at night, he told me, he went to school, working toward a high school diploma.

The flush of the physical work, the adventure involved in doing the kind of apprentice work novelists were supposed to be doing—everything conspired to make me feel easy, free, good. The coal car was adrift, the noises of the factory were distant.

About a third of the factory workers at Chevrolet-Indianapolis were black, most of them in the lowest salary categories, and most of the white workers, their origins in Kentucky, Tennessee, and southern Indiana, hated them. (The Indiana Ku Klux Klan had had its headquarters in Indianapolis in the twenties.) The workers all seemed to have a special hatred for those blacks who had recently come from the South. "Even their own kind don't like them niggers," they'd tell me. Until those months in Indianapolis I had only read about the sign I began to see there everywhere—in bars, motels, restaurants, amusement parks: WE SOLICIT WHITE PATRONAGE ONLY. If such signs, attitudes, were prevalent in a northern city in 1960, my imagination was able to confirm its worst beliefs about the South, about what things had been like for blacks in all the years before 1960.

Our talk that day in the coal car was generally easy —about sports, the factory, living in "Naptown." He was from Louisiana, and when I asked him how he'd gotten as far north as Indianapolis, he told the story quickly, without changing the level of his voice. His grandfather, his father, his older brothers had all worked in a factory in his home town, owned by a white man. After dropping out of high school, he'd worked there also. A few years before—when he'd been about seventeen—the owner had accused him of stealing. "I didn't do it, man, and I told him so. He kept yelling at me I did it and I kept telling him to yell at somebody else, I didn't do the fucking thing. When I got home that night my old man took a strap to me. I told him I didn't do it, but he strapped me anyway. 'Don't you be talking back to a white man,' he said, and my brothers just ate their meal and didn't say nothing. The next morning I took my money and got on a bus and come north."

That was all. We worked the rest of the day, and I remember that, like other workers, he offered me a ride home. As always, I accepted. We'd stop, as we did that day, in a bar along the way for some beers, and the guys would release cursing, stories, shoptalk of a kind I didn't often hear in the factory. "This the color skin God give me," he said at one point, angrily shoving his muscled forearm in front of my eyes. "If any man don't like it, that's his tough shit. It's mine, see—? A man wants to be my friend, that's fine with me. He don't, that's okay too."

Another worker I became friendly with was a millwright—a kind of jack-of-all-trades, earning the highest hourly salary in the plant—and we were assigned to "troubleshoot" a row of presses. I worked with him for about a week. He had a reputation among the workers for being a "character." Just to have him walk by was enough to make most of them shake their heads and chuckle. He sang "My Old Kentucky Home" off-key, endlessly; he goosed any worker who didn't see him coming; he started wetted-down paper towel fights in the toilets.

The favorite part of his repertoire came at the end of a day's work. After putting his holster and tools away, he'd begin to edge toward the punch-out clock. All eyes would be on him. His own eyes would move this way and that, wary, on the lookout for his foreman, and when the siren went off and the mad rush took place to get in line and punch out, he'd always be first. After he'd rung out, he'd stand with me and chide the other workers, still in line, for "doing overtime."

He was a wiry little man, a plug of tobacco set in his cheek. He had his own home, outside Indianapolis, and two daughters, the oldest of whom (at sixteen), he told me, had just been "knocked up." "You're lucky," he said to me on my last day as his helper. "You won't have to do this kind of shit when you get to be my age." We'd finished washing up, with the usual horsing around, and for no apparent reason, as if he thought I might appreciate an explanation: "They expect me to be their clown, so I'm their clown."

And a bit later, over beers: "Even if you're a skilled worker like me, what do you have to look forward to in life? Same stuff, day-in, day-out, and maybe the union gets you a raise in pay every couple years. But nothing really changes, you know what I mean? You're lucky, kid— you take good care of yourself."

My friendliness with some of the workers in the plant led to my first and only run-in with my superiors. One day I was summoned from the factory to Ralph's office; he told me that he'd heard that I'd been riding to and from work with "hourlies."

"We all think it would be a good idea if you wouldn't," he said. "Do you understand what I'm saying to you, Jay?"

I nodded, but I made no promises—and I continued, afterwards, to ride home with the guy from Louisiana, and with other "hourlies." Ralph could tell I didn't like the "advice" he'd had to give me, and he tried to soften it by explaining that it would make my own position—and that of the workers—so much more difficult someday if I were, say, to become foreman of a man I'd been riding home with. I remained silent.

The interview ended with the information that, over and above the commonsense reasons for not riding home, for not becoming "too friendly" with hourlies, plant policy forbade it. "An executive," one of the GM pamphlets I'd read that first week had stated, "has a lot in common with a jockey, a racing driver or a fighter pilot. They all have the same job—to get maximum performance from the machine, animate or inanimate, that has been entrusted to their care."

At the end of the summer I accepted an invitation

from one of the other trainees, Mike McComas, to rent an apartment with him. He made all the arrangements, and in mid-September we moved into a newly furnished four-room place in The Meadows. The Meadows was a new development on the north side of Indianapolis— "niggers ain't got this far north yet," neighbors were to tell me—composed of parking areas, gardens, and several dozen modern three-storey red-brick buildings.

Most of the residents were young executives, school-teachers, career girls; there were a lot of young divorcees (more than I'd imagined existed), a few young married couples. Mike and I got along well; he was the only one of the young executives who made jokes about the nature of organization life. I was civil in my dealings with our neighbors; but generally I preferred, at the end of a day's work, to stay by myself. I read, I took walks back and forth across the empty field that joined our development to the Meadows Shopping Center. I drank, I ate. I telephoned Ginny, I accrued a mild quantity of guilt by getting involved with some of the local girls, I waited for the weekends.

The Meadows, too, was a mistake, and I knew it the first night I arrived. Ginny and I had moved my belongings there in her car from Ralph's mother's house, and as we drove up to my new home, we both saw our welcoming symbol, looked at each other, shrugged, then laughed: one of the young executives was standing on the front lawn, his arms around a girl, showing her how to swing a golf club.

On the outside, things were going better than ever. For the first time in my life, I began to have extra money in my pocket, and I used it. I bought the books, clothes, and records I wanted; I ate in restaurants; I went to bowling alleys several times a week; I went to any movie I wanted; Mike and I prided ourselves on the orgiastic meals we'd prepare every evening—huge porterhouse steaks, a pound each of shrimp cocktail—and within six months I would gain over twenty pounds.

I became dulled, dull; on weekends I'd sit and watch football games on TV all day Saturday and Sunday, Ginny sitting next to me, neither of us speaking to one another. I'd apologize afterwards, but I didn't change. Among the other young executives at The Meadows I soon developed—for the first time in my life—a reputation as a "shy, quiet guy." I still wanted to do only one thing —write novels—and GM was supposed to be the means to that end, but after a day's work at the factory I found myself spent, without even the energy to approach my typewriter.

The only writing I did during those first few months were the mad exhortations I scribbled in the margins of my paperback copy of William Whyte's *The Organization Man.* (In the margins of Chapter I: "Oh the horror! the horror!" "Define!" "Yes!" "Don't grandiloquize the pathetic." "No!" "Never! to make the best of the worst of all possible worlds is not to disarm! @ best: to endure!" etcetera.)

As if Whyte's book were a text in literary criticism, I fought him line by line, wrote critiques at the ends of each chapter. I was absolute and academic, and I was enraged. His "Introduction" ended with the following paragraph:

> There are only a few times in organization life when he [the Organization Man] can wrench his destiny into his own hands—and if he does not fight then, he will make a surrender that will later mock him. But when is that time? Will he know the time when he sees it? By what standards is he to judge? He does feel an obligation to the group; he does sense moral constraints on his free will. If he goes against the group, is he being courageous

—or just stubborn? Helpful—or selfish? Is he, as he so often wonders, right after all? It is in the resolution of a multitude of such dilemmas, I submit, that the real issue of individualism lies today.

To which I replied, scornfully:

Wrong: your piecemeal individualism is pathetic in face of actual horror: of 5 day a week, 8 hours a day, 50 weeks, 45 year careers.

Your organization man (as above) is already an imbecile—i.e., feeble-minded.

You don't worship: but you do worse: accept.

Given the modern org: there can be no individualism [my def] because no self-expression, no creativity. Spasmodic assertion of individuality vs. brotherly coercion are like whimpers of dying cats.

The most famous part of Whyte's book—students at Columbia and Indiana had referred to it often, had seen in it a brilliant satire—was an "Appendix" on entrance requirements for those wanting to become organization men. It was titled "How to Cheat on Personality Tests" and Whyte's point was the obvious one: large corporations wanted their young executives to be stable conformists—obedient, cheerful, kind, clean, neat, etc. Whyte told you how to "cheat" (since we were all, it seemed, nonconformists and idealists at heart) so that you could get into the organization. "Don't be too dominant," "Incline to conservatism," "Don't split hairs," ". . . there does seem to be one moral: don't think too much," etc.

What drove me crazy—what elicited more scribblings—was that Whyte refused to recognize what was, for me, the point of the tests (several of which I'd taken): GM and the rest did not want as a junior executive any young man who was not intelligent enough to see through the tests, to know the answers the corpora-

MY BLESSING NOT MY DOOM

tion was looking for. I.e., the Organization *wanted* cheaters. The tests were the young organization man's initiation into his new life. Everybody knew the kind of answers wanted, the kind of behavior deemed acceptable; everybody laughed with Whyte at the tests, at all the games in which nobody really believed—but everybody went along with them. This was all that mattered, I wrote. Whyte's Ayn Rand-ish notion that the thing for young men to do was to cheat on the tests, get into the corporation and *then* inject new life into it ("resist" the Organization), seemed to me totally insane.

Cheating (compromise) was required from the start, and the first time you refused to cheat, the first time you tried, in any important way, to be an individualist, you would fail in the company's eyes. Nobody could question basic assumptions, values, and get ahead; one was only free to make things more efficient, more profitably benevolent—one was free to reform the "blandness" of organization life.

I remember, for example, being called into Ralph's office and being given an IBM card on which a deduction from my salary had already been programmed. The deduction was for the annual United Fund charity drive; our Plant Manager, Ralph explained, was one of the drive chairmen for the Indianapolis area. Ralph asked, with a pleasant laugh, if I wanted to contribute to this charity the amount which had already been deducted and he gave me a printed card showing how the amount each person contributed was scaled to his salary.

"And if I say no?" I asked.

Ralph shrugged, smiled: "You'll lose your job."

We both laughed at that. I thought for a second, then: "You mean it, don't you?" I said.

He nodded. "Yes. That's right, but . . ."

"All right," I said, and I okayed the deduction.

Whyte was on the side of the Corporation (he merely
wanted to improve it from within), and I railed at him for
page after page because, I suppose, I had discovered that
I was not.

When, in the last paragraph of the last chapter,
Whyte declared that the organization man "must *fight*
The Organization," I replied in capitals, "NO—He must
leave the Org."

In the margins of his book, I was quickly becoming a
pamphleteer: the System was all-powerful, it could not be
changed, reformed from within; therefore, I explained to
Whyte again and again, it had to be overthrown. My feelings were those of an anarchist—tinged with Marxism: all
my sympathies were with the workers. The thrill I felt at
the idea of working "on the line" told me that I had entered the training program still believing in the union
man, still believing that there was something inherently
more *real* about physical work and poor people than
about intellectual work, the lives of middle- and upper-
class people.

My sympathies stayed with the workers (and against
"the bosses") even though I saw, too quickly, that any
ideal notion of The Working Man I'd held had been
based on romance, wish, myth. The men in the factory
were, by and large, bigoted, lazy, uninteresting. Their desires were identical to the desires of those who worked in
the executive wing of the plant: they wanted more money
to buy more goods; they seemed to want no say in what
was produced or how it was produced.

They were profoundly conservative politically: anything that threatened, or that they thought—were taught
—threatened the relative stability of their jobs, their lives
(e.g., poor people, black people, smart-aleck professors,
beatniks) was to be derided, kept down. Jokes about
"niggers" and "kikes" were the staple of their humor; hate

sheets were often shown to me for my approval; veterans of the Second World War, not knowing I was Jewish, would tell me that the only mistake we'd made at the end of the war was "not to join up with the Nazis against the Commies."

During my months in the factory, I heard, a half-dozen to a dozen times, conversations which began—"I'm not saying Hitler should of had all those camps—but maybe a lot of them Jews had it coming to them. . . ."

Workers would tell me stories about the times they'd gone "coon-huntin" on Saturday nights when they were young—four or five guys, with chains, riding dark southern roads and looking for a young black guy. Others told me about the homes—of blacks who'd moved into their neighborhoods—they'd broken windows in, torn the plumbing from, burned down.

The force with which anger rose in me was jolting; but I felt helpless to reply, to do anything. My satisfactions were slim. Once, driving home from work, I nearly killed a group of us by cracking the driver over the head with a rolled-up newspaper for calling me a "nigger-lover." Another time, after spending a day with a foreman who seemed to find my presence at his side the occasion for eight hours of nigger-cursing, I thanked him, shook his hand, and informed him that my mother was Negro.

For the most part, during my days at the factory, I was on my own. Although some foremen and executives I was assigned to made efforts to educate me concerning their departments, most of them regarded my assignment to them as a nuisance. As soon as I thought that they felt they'd discharged their duties by giving me a half-hour or an hour rundown on what went on in their office, their assembly line, I'd generally tell them that I knew they had enough to worry about without me, and that I'd just as soon roam around on my own. If there were any work they needed done, I'd be available—and if I had any questions I assured them I'd ask.

They were usually pleased with this deal. Thus, though I spent many days doing tedious, menial work— taking time-motion studies, running off blueprints, working simple machines and presses—I spent an equal number of days doing nothing. Nobody seemed to mind, or notice. I walked around with a serious, concerned look on my face, and thought of escape.

One of my favorite time-passing activities was to find a desk somewhere and read through minutes of labor-management hearings. Some of the stories (the causes for grievances, suspensions) were good, and I would spend hours typing out those which interested me. One, I thought, would be the basis for my next novel—and I planned to begin the novel with a reprint of a grievance procedure: the case concerned an Irish worker who was accused of starting a wildcat strike. What fascinated me were the accounts—amid bureaucratic jargon—of the man's prodigious drinking abilities. The document listed the bars he drank at, the amounts he drank, the things he reportedly said to workers.

I found other pastimes. During my time in the machine-repair shop, I helped the men with what they referred to as their "government projects"—tool chests for themselves, toys for their kids, knicknacks to bring home. I learned to work some of the machines, and I made myself several letter openers (steel blades, lucite handles). I enjoyed one of the games the workers in machine-repair taught me: to demonstrate the strength and thickness of the sheet metal being used to make truck bodies, one worker would hold a piece of the steel while another worker would see if he could pierce the sheet in one stroke with a nail (or letter opener). At the assembly plants, I was told, there were inspectors whose sole job was to check for workers' "playfulness" (sabotage): tools under the hood, cigarettes in the fuel line, etc.

Some of the older workers would sometimes tell me stories about what things had been like in the days before the unions had power. The stories were out of Dos Passos —police disrupting rallies, union organizers losing jobs— and I loved them. Several of the workers remembered the time when, after breaking up a union rally across from the plant (before it was Chevrolet-Indianapolis it had been a carriage factory), Indianapolis police had cornered the speechmakers and beaten them senseless while the workers looked on.

Though I was well aware of all the goldbricking that went on because of the union, and though I knew to my disappointment that the union itself had given up the desire to have any say about what was made in the factory, I found myself remaining more impressed by what the situation would have been had there been no unions.

For me, the harried, frantic, sour dispositions of most shop foremen accurately reflected the nature of things: a man at the lowest level of management, being in the most precarious position (there were no unions for foremen), had to peck hardest at those under him if he expected to get ahead, to keep his job.

The Working Class sensibilities which swelled in my chest, the feelings of hostility I developed toward my Employer—I seemed to have no trouble controlling them. I did my job, I was friendly to all, I remained in favor; I was able to grasp the functions of departments and workers quickly, and the reports I wrote were considered excellent . . . "The function of the Personnel Department is to process and care for all the personnel, hourly and salaried, employed at Chevrolet-Indianapolis. This involves

many activities. . . ." The progress report on me which
was sent to Detroit at the end of my first three months
gave me the highest possible rating.

Away from the factory, I began to retreat more
deeply into myself; I hated and feared the people around
me—especially the young people at The Meadows—I despised them, for reasons that weren't, even at the time,
difficult to figure out, more than I believed possible, and I
began to deal with my fears and hatreds by waging my
own silent and private wars.

The newspapers I read every day became ready—
and impersonal—targets. The two major Indianapolis papers, the *News* and *Star*, were both owned by the same
man, Eugene C. Pulliam, and were both conservative. I
was able that fall, in the factory, at The Meadows, to debate the relative merits of Nixon and Kennedy, but I felt
lost when it came to arguing against the editorial pages
of these papers. Here, the views of the people around me
were trapped up in a rhetoric I found baffling; thus, an
editorial in the *Indianapolis News*, of November 21, 1960,
against school desegregation:

TRAGEDY IN NEW ORLEANS

The tragedy which has gripped the city of New Or-
leans is grim testimony to what men can do when they
try to coerce one another into virtue.

. . . The stated object of school integration is to pro-
mote the welfare of the Negro in the South. But what has
in fact happened? The real result has been to marshal
economic pressures against Negroes, to inflame latent
prejudice, to incite racial violence. Moreover, it would
seem the integration effort has not achieved the explicit
point on which the entire struggle has been staked . . .

. . . The end of discrimination, in the psychological
sense which so concerned the [Supreme] court, can
come only when the white people of the South want it to

come. If they do not want it there is no way to force them into willing compliance . . .

In dealing with this kind of argument, where could one begin? Still, I began: I discovered that I would, day after day, when I got home from work, struggle to refute the logic, to probe the assumptions, to devastate the reasoning that exemplified and sustained all I was beginning to feel was wrong with the world.

Little in my first twenty-one years had prepared me for the America I was living in, or for my reactions to it. In New York, if I'd even given it any thought, I'd probably comforted myself with the notion that there existed in the world an efficient division of labor: I worked on novels, "somebody else" worked against injustice. In Indianapolis, though, nobody seemed to be working against injustice—and everybody seemed unjust. The feeling was obsessive, ferocious: if I didn't do something to fight the evil (the people) around me, nobody would.

What was wrong in the factory, in The Meadows, seemed to me to be preserved—paralleled, reinforced—by the rhetoric of the *Indianapolis News* and *Star*. Support for segregation, for Trujillo, for invasion ("liberation") of Cuba, for a Monroe Doctrine for Africa—that most people I met in Indianapolis did not seem to feel that these positions were extreme ones only made their extremity seem more terrible to me.

In the fall of 1960 I found a particular, and personal, opponent—a man I'd never heard of before I'd read the Indianapolis papers. His syndicated columns seemed to speak most directly to the people around me, for their way of seeing things. His columns reflected what was for me an impenetrable double standard in which morality and self-interest were used not only to justify one another, but were confused, sincerely, as far as I could tell —which made matters worse, *for* one another.

I read the columns religiously, copied out paragraphs, debated them—but the more I did so, the less
capable I became of reason or reasonableness.

> We would hold on to Africa, in part because West-
> ern survival there is essential to victory over Commun-
> ism, but no less than because we know that the privilege
> of being born in the West carries with it the responsibil-
> ity of extending our good fortune to others.
>
> We are the bearers of Western Civilization—the
> most noble product of the heart and mind of man. If, in
> Africa, the West has failed in the past to do the full mea-
> sure of its duty, then all the more reason for doing our
> duty now.
>
> Justice is a worthy objective, but if justice for the
> Bantus entails driving the government of the Union of
> South Africa away from the West, then the Bantus must
> be prepared to carry their identification cards yet awhile
> longer.

Under the press of my GM experiences, the doubts I
had about extending the benefits of Western Civilization
to the rest of the world were severe enough; the belief
that these benefits were to be imposed forcibly on others
by us, and the fact that such a belief did not seem, to
those who held it, incompatible with beliefs in "freedom,"
in the "right to self-determination," etc., left me furious—
and incapable of argument.

Moreover, the way in which such columns continually, easily spoke of using military power to bring about
such benefits terrified me.

> Only in one instance have we moved purposefully
> and effectively to dislodge existing Communist power—
> in Guatemala. And contrary to what has been said re-
> cently, we did not wait for "outside pressures" and
> "world opinion" to bring down the Communist govern-
> ment.

As everyone knows [I did not, until then], we moved decisively to effect an anti-Communist coup d'état and there is no need to apologize for what we did. We served our national interests and by so doing we saved the Guatemalan people the ultimate in human misery.

Do you believe that, confronted with the incontrovertible fact of American superior military might, Khrushchev would risk World War III over Egypt or Africa or any other piece of geography far removed from the Russian homeland?

We should be prepared, I suggest, to exploit our present power advantage in every area of the world threatened by Communist subversion.

True disarmament will be possible only when, one, Russian Communism has been destroyed as a world force or, two, Russian Communism renounces its avowed purpose of world conquest. Since the second condition would most certainly mean the first condition has been fulfilled, isn't it time that we in America put aside wishful thinking and took up the business of defending freedom?

The columns were written by Barry Goldwater, and I was amazed that there could even be a United States Senator who held such beliefs. I began to suspect that I was the one who'd grown up in the provinces.

I thought of giving it all up—the job, my writing, my girlfriend—to join the Freedom Rides which were taking place at the time, but I didn't. My political activities and education remained private, and I seemed to like it that way. The longer my thoughts remained unspoken, the more special they seemed to become. I don't recall ever trying to talk with anyone in Indianapolis about anything serious.

I remember, sitting in my living room at The Meadows, the noises of a party from next door blasting through the walls, seeing Malcolm X on television for the first time. Believing deeply in Martin Luther King's nonviolent campaigns, I had been prepared to despise Malcolm —the spokesman, I'd been taught, for a violent black extremism which paralleled that of the KKK. One thing he said reached me: for black Americans to use their bodies to march, to petition from white people for what should already have been theirs could be described in only one word—"begging." And Afro-Americans, Malcolm said, should not be beggars.

In the fall and winter of 1960–61, the Indianapolis papers were denouncing James Baldwin—William Buckley, I recall, making an invidious comparison between him and Adolf Eichmann—and Martin Luther King as irresponsible extremists. If I found, then, that Malcolm's description of things seemed true, where did that leave me?

My way of seeing things, I noticed, came more and more from the black man's point of view. If you were black, I reasoned, what good was the right to vote, the right to protest, the right to free speech—even when such rights existed—when the law of the land was the law of the majority, and when this majority was white? If you could not convince even the most enlightened and best-intentioned of men (e.g., New Yorkers who read the *Times* and *Post*) that it was both immoral and impractical to counsel moderation, what chance would there ever be to convince the American People (e.g., my neighbors and colleagues in Indianapolis) that things should be changed?

The appeal to work through the orderly democratic processes began to sound to me like just another way in which bigotry, injustice, and the status quo would be preserved. New York was not America, Indianapolis was

—and in America, I concluded, the possession of power determined all.

I read voraciously, seeking out and discovering writers who agreed with such thoughts, who could articulate my sense of things. My bibles that fall and winter were C. Wright Mills's *Listen Yankee* and *The Causes of World War III*, Aldous Huxley's *Brave New World Revisited*, Edward Sapir's essays in *Language Culture and Personality*, and some essays by a man I'd never heard of, Paul Goodman, which were appearing in *Commentary* magazine (and which would later become part of *Growing Up Absurd*).

By the end of my fourth month at Chevrolet-Indianapolis, I had paid off my debt to the Business Men's Clearing House, and I began to believe that escape was a genuine possibility. By this time, and for the rest of my days at GM, I was also, while I walked the aisles of the factory, talking to myself: cursing, analyzing, theorizing, plotting revolution.

Nobody around me—executives or union men— seemed to feel that the hours spent inside the plant were too high a price to pay for what the money earned during those hours could purchase. The few times that I made faint suggestions to the contrary, people looked at me as if I were crazy. So I read, I talked to myself, I constructed theories, I lived well, ate well, put away money —and began to fear that I was, quite literally, going mad. More: as the split between the outward progress of my life and the inner tumbling grew, I sensed the dividends that madness would have to offer: attention, drama, escape, sympathy . . . if I could not write a new novel, I could, at least, become a character for one.

It was not that things grew worse during my months at GM; they didn't, really—but the duration of my confused feelings, of the conditions which provoked them—

these wore me down. Feelings of sickness and rage alter-
nated with feelings of impotence and hostility. Inside, the
effect was violent, terrifying. If what was good for
General Motors was good for the country, then they were
both in need of revolution. Without it, I told myself, we
were all doomed.

At the time there was, for me, only one truth: that if
the price paid for having cars was the work done at the
factory for the better part of a man's life, then the only
hope for mankind was in a world without cars.

The thought was exhilarating; the moral (*Destroy*—!)
thrilling. In my mind, the world came to be constructed
—driven—by what were abstract, allegorical forces: Racism, Capitalism, Industrialism, Imperialism, The System,
The Status Quo, Ignorance. What I had said to Whyte
became more and more true: all compromise was error.
You could not make life on the assembly line more
humane—you had to destroy the assembly line.

I copied out, at the time, passages from an essay by
Edward Sapir and carried them with me. That Sapir had
written the essay ("Culture, Genuine and Spurious") in
1924—and that, as I thought, nobody now knew about
it—made its truth more powerful, my possession of it
more beautiful:

> The major activities of the individual must directly
> satisfy his own creative and emotional impulses . . .
> [They] must always be something more than a means to
> an end. The great cultural fallacy of industrialism, as de-
> veloped up to the present time, is that in harnessing ma-
> chines to our uses it has not known how to avoid the har-
> nessing of the majority of mankind to its machines. The
> telephone girl who lends her capacities, during the
> greater part of the living day, to the manipulation of a
> technical routine that has an eventually high efficiency
> value but that answers to no spiritual needs of her own is

an appalling sacrifice to civilization. As a solution of the problem of culture she is a failure—the more dismal the greater her natural endowment. As with the telephone girl, so, it is to be feared, with the great majority of us, slave-stokers to fires that burn for demons we would destroy, were it not that they appear in the guise of our benefactors.

. . . No harmony and depth of life, no culture, is possible when activity is well-nigh circumscribed by the sphere of immediate ends and when functioning within that sphere is so fragmentary as to have no inherent intelligibility or interest. Here lies the grimmest joke of our present American civilization. The vast majority of us, deprived of any but an insignificant and culturally abortive share in the satisfaction of the immediate wants of mankind, are further deprived of both opportunity and stimulation to share in the production of non-utilitarian values. Part of the time we are dray horses; the rest of the time we are listless consumers of goods which have received no least impress of our personality. In other words, our spiritual selves go hungry, for the most part, pretty much all of the time.

What seems fascinating to me now—and pleasantly so—is how much more real than reality the written and printed word was to me during my last months at General Motors. Books, articles, letters, company literature— they seemed to have engaged, aroused, depressed, and enraged me more than people or events. Unable to write, the writing of others became all important, all powerful. Quotes from Sapir or Mills or Goldwater would, for days at a time, become the most important parts of my life—I would carry them with me until, without having tried, I would find that I could recite them aloud, almost verbatim.

The most significant piece of writing for me during

that time was a company pamphlet which I picked up from the information rack at the exit to the factory on my way out one day. It was entitled "My Blessing Not My Doom," and it was "Published For GM Men And Women" by the "Information Rack Service, General Motors Personnel Staff." (Ralph—and his superior, the Director of Personnel—knowing I had been an English major, and praising me for the quality of my reports—had suggested that I might someday work in this division of GM.) The titles in the racks changed regularly—"What We Must Know About Communism," "Handbook of First Aid," "The Untold Story of OUR FLAG," "Easy Ways to Better English," "How Reliable is 99.9%?"—and I used most of them for toilet-reading. This one, however, even more than *The Organization Man* or the editorial pages of the *News* and *Star*, possessed me.

It began with the proposition that "people need work almost as badly as they need food; without it they're devoured by restlessness and discontent." A few paragraphs later: "Realizing that you actually enjoy working is part of growing up. But many people never learn it; they never achieve the peace of mind and contentment this knowledge brings. They spend their lives in a prison where work is the eternal punishment.

> Others wake up to the fact that they like to work only when the time comes to retire. As their daily job comes to an end, they suddenly realize how much it has meant to them, and what a vacuum will be left in their lives without it. Then they belatedly try to develop hobbies and pursuits that will keep them active.

The central section of the pamphlet advanced the major argument:

> How can we avoid the feeling of compulsion that makes work a burden? To some extent, we can't escape it. Most of us have to work for a living. There's no use

trying to kid ourselves about that. Nevertheless, there are two things anyone can do to take the edge off the feeling of compulsion and make his job more pleasant.

One is to do *more* work and *better* work than you have to. Don't do only as much work as you have to. Do *more!* Don't do work that is barely good enough to get by. Do *better* work than you have to. Do the best job you know how.

"That idea," some people will snort, "is strictly for the birds." But it isn't. It's practical. Take a look around you and judge the truth of it for yourself. To whom does work seem a greater drudgery, to those who do only as much as they are forced to do, or to those who throw themselves into the job and do more than they have to?

Why does a good workman fret when there isn't enough work to be done? Because he finds it more tiring to work half-heartedly than to work hard. He knows the day is longer when he tries to goldbrick. And the end of the day leaves him with no warming sense of accomplishment.

The man who does only as much as he has to turns his job into a prison. Compulsion hangs over every move that he makes. Everything he does, he does only because he is forced to do it.

Here there was a drawing: a worker, bent over, is unhappy at his machine—a machine which punches an endless series of holes in an endless strip of metal. He is frowning. Tied to his leg is a ball and chain. Two policemen, with rifles, stand guard on either side of him.

The man who does more than he has to clears the walls of this prison in a single bound. He does whatever he is doing not because he has to but because he wants to. He is working of his own free will. Compulsion has been left behind.

Another drawing: the same worker is at the same press, only now he is smiling as the sheet of punched holes moves rapidly along. There are no policemen. His ball and chain lie in a nearby trash basket.

This may seem like a subtle mental distinction. But it's real. You can see it reflected in the happiness and satisfaction—or lack of it—in those around you.

The second way to circumvent a feeling of compulsion in your job is to realize this fact: even if you didn't *have* to work, you would probably *want* to work anyway.

If you don't believe this, stop and think a moment. If you didn't work, what could you possibly do with yourself? Would you like to join the idle rich? Study their faces sometime. Do they reflect peace and contentment? They are the most bored and empty people on earth.

Can you think of any adult who doesn't work whom you believe to be happy? I can't. Countless men—born rich—have spent millions of dollars to buy or create enterprises in which they could have the pleasure of working. They could not stand a purposeless, workless existence.

We need work desperately. We need it to absorb our mental and physical energies. If these energies are not expended in constructive fashion, they turn inward and poison our minds and bodies with restlessness and dissatisfaction.

We need work to give us a feeling of being needed, wanted and useful. We also need it to have balance to our lives; without work, rest and relaxation have no meaning.

The pamphlet ended with the narrator's reminiscence:

People who think they don't like to work remind me of an officer I knew in the Navy. For four years he griped about everything connected with the Navy. Then when the time came to get out—he signed up for four more years.

Don't wait until you retire to realize you like to work. *Start enjoying your job today!*

I was obsessed by the pamphlet (in the years since, I've used it in every English class I've ever taught—junior high school, high school, college—still trying to account for its hold on me, for the feelings it was once able to arouse), and I brought it back to the factory with me on subsequent days, showing it to the workers I knew. They would laugh at it, then shake their heads, and admit that even though the pamphlet had "the same old bullshit" in it that all the others did, there was "a lot of truth" in this one. Again—and this seemed to me the most terrible thing—even though they admitted that there was a lot of truth in it, they continued to laugh.

My life became increasingly interior. As it did, I told myself that I was at last doing what my father had always wanted me to do: I was, with a vengeance, reading the front pages of the newspaper before the sports pages. More than this, I was, if only in my mind, developing a social and political consciousness, social and political theories.

At the least, I told myself, I was, for the first time in my life doing something I'd never done before: I was questioning, not a particular policy or action, but what I perceived of as the system underlying that policy or action.

The logic and reason with which I supported my call to revolution seemed to me irrefutable—and the theory I evolved at the time became, for many years and through many actual political activities, my working hypothesis. In basic outline, it went as follows: men could not perform inhuman tasks eight hours a day for the better part of their waking lives and live meaningful human lives in the time which was left over. It was absurd to put one's faith in the men who possessed the power to work change, whether in industry, unions, or politics, for even the best of them were concerned only with matters of expediency. They might object to certain forms of injustice, they might work to correct certain problems, but none of them questioned the basic assumptions, structures upon which, within which, everything was built. Rather the opposite: they questioned, and sought to change, in order to reinforce the system, to sustain the status quo.

Everyone, I believed, sold and defended the products of whatever company he happened to work for. If and when one changed companies one did the same for the new employer, and this loyalty was named morality. If one meant to succeed, and all those with the power to work change had obviously meant to, one criticized, one initiated changes only when these would lead to greater stability, to expansion, to the furtherance of self-interest.

For a man to have spent years working his way up in a corporation and to have retained by the time he reached the top any kind of radical vision, he would have to have harbored in his day-to-day encounters during those years, a schizophrenic state of mind that would have made the split which was developing in mine seem, by comparison, nonexistent.

Moreover, the situation was critical precisely because those I worked with enjoyed the benefits of life that I felt should be shared by all men—decent salary, good working conditions, leisure time, adequate food, clothing, shelter—; they would, it followed, do everything within their power (and they were the ones *with* power) to resist those forces which threatened, or which they thought threatened, their way of life. There was nothing specifically wrong with a new car every third or fourth year, or a house in suburbia, except that there seemed to me to be a direct, inevitable relation between the affluence such things represented and the lack of them in the poor parts of Mississippi, New York, Brazil, South Africa, India, et al. (In 1965, speaking to American troops in Korea, Lyndon Johnson was to sum up what I'd been getting at: "Don't forget," he told the soldiers, "there are only two hundred million of us in the world of three billion. They want what we've got, and we're not going to give it to them.")

The devil, as I perceived it, was inertia: nobody in a position to change things would dare question, for example, what seemed to me most important: the quality of daily life involved in the jobs most men worked at—they would only question (as Kennedy and Nixon did in their TV debates that fall) how *many* jobs were needed to keep an economy moving. The good will of honest men, liberal reforms, etcetera—as good as some of these might be in themselves, they only maintained the illusion of progress, the hope that all change was possible through the systems, the leaders available. The opposite seemed true: specific reforms only helped minimize discontent, only came into being to gird, to strengthen what I perceived of as The System. The System itself caused suffering, injustice, oppression, waste; it was, literally and figuratively, destroying lives—and, since it contained the seeds of its own preservation, would continue to do so. Immediate and revolutionary transformation, therefore, was imperative. Without it, I said to myself again and again, we were all doomed.

My desire to write was in imminent danger. As with other Americans, so with me; the impulse to preserve one's property and one's way of life was the most powerful and conservative of forces: I did what I had to—the only thing I could do—I decided to take the advice I'd written in the margins of *The Organization Man*.

One morning, a week before Christmas, 1960, I went in to see Ralph and I told him that I was, as of that day, resigning. I decided ahead of time that I would not give him any of my new political theories, but that I would try

—as I did—to let him think that it was simply that some
people were "cut out for the business world," and that
others were not. I cited my liberal arts background, I revealed to him the fact that I was an unpublished novelist.
He was disappointed in my decision, sympathetic; he told
me that I was due for a sizeable raise in salary in another
week, the end of the first six months of the training program, and that another even larger increase would come
at the end of the year. He urged me to reconsider, told
me how much I was liked by everybody, tried to find out
why I felt the way I did, why I'd made the decision.

He seemed honestly puzzled, sincere—and I felt,
inevitably, some personal loyalty to him for all he'd done
for me. I started to try to explain some of the feelings I'd
experienced during my six months at Chevrolet-Indianapolis. I wanted him to *understand*—but when I mentioned
the lack of personal satisfaction I felt due to the fact that
I helped to make only one part of a truck, due to the fact
that I'd had no say in deciding what kind of truck it was
that I helped make the part for, he became bewildered.

What happened next seemed surreal: he looked out
the window, and as he did a Chevrolet car was passing
by—Ralph smiled, pointed to it, nodded affirmatively:
"Whenever I see a car go by that has a part in it that
came out of our plant, Jay," he said, "I feel a tremendous
sense of pride—"

The discussion seemed, already, to be taking place
somewhere else; but he asked me more questions and I
answered them. I told him, as briefly as I could, trying
not to seem strange or to hurt his feelings, about my reactions to assembly lines, to stamping presses. I had prepared the sentence ahead of time: "I guess I just can't be
the one—the agent—that tells the men to press two buttons all day long as efficiently as they can." To which he
replied, as I must have known he would, a slightly puz-

zled expression on his face, a question (which proved the justice of all my analyses, of all my theories) implicit in his statement: "But if you don't do it, someone else will anyway—"

I didn't—couldn't—argue. "The way I look at it, Jay," he went on, leaning toward me, "we're making life easier for them. They're happy. Most of them aren't fit to do anything better anyway. . . ."

FOUR: *A Letter to Kennedy*

Once when Mary George was thirteen and he was
five, she had lured him with the promise of an un-
named present into a large tent full of people and
had dragged him backwards up to the front where
a man in a blue suit and red and white tie was
standing. "Here," she said in a loud voice. "I'm already saved but you can save him. He's a real
stinker and too big for his britches." He had broken her grip and shot out of there like a small cur
and later when he had asked for his present, she
had said, "You would have got Salvation if you
had waited for it but since you acted the way you
did, you get nothing!"

— Flannery O'Connor. "The Enduring Chill."

Walking the aisles of the factory, keeping to myself
at The Meadows, driving back and forth to Bloomington—I became as fiercely moral and absolute as the
most fundamentalist of Midwest reactionaries. I was alone
—and different; different from all those around me because what I desired derived from something other
than self-interest. My reasoning traveled its own circuit:
novels were useless because major political changes were
necessary; but the emotions which told me that these
changes were necessary were not themselves political,

they were moral and human. Precisely because such emotions should, in the forms (in the environment) I was experiencing them, have been the basis for fiction, I could not, in conscience, make them the matter of my novels.

Novels were a luxury suited to another era: I had a moral duty, I felt, to give up my fiction, and to devote all my energies to changing the conditions of the real world which surrounded me . . . I had to do this, in fact, so that a sacrifice such as mine would not, in some future time, be necessary. I convinced myself, in short, that I had to give up novels for politics; that such a decision (such a sacrifice) was necessary, I told myself, was the clearest sign of the urgency—and tragedy—of the times.

By the time I'd left GM, I'd convinced myself that I had to fight not only against everything the factory and corporation and The Meadows represented, or against Barry Goldwater and the *News* and *Star*—but against a greater danger, one which I perceived as flowing from the same force of inertia as the rest—I had to fight against the possibility of nuclear war.

I don't remember exactly when my mind made this leap, shifted its focus in this way. Perhaps it was simply that I noticed that those who supported the things I found most vile in my immediate environment, also seemed willing, always, to risk everybody else's life in order to maintain such things. There really were millions of ordinary, reasonable Americans who loved their own children and hated the children of others, and who believed, and were ready to act on the belief, that we were all better dead than red.

Like the *News* and *Star*, nuclear war was an impersonal target. I could be moved by the views or the plight of an individual I knew, or by the death, in a southern church, of black children I did not know—but how did one relate personally to the possibility of hundreds of millions of simultaneous deaths? One related, as I was soon to discover, with passionate abstraction.

What was clear at the time was that all other problems were insignificant when compared to the prospect of nuclear war. To work on a novel, to argue against a racist, a newspaper, a politician—these were luxuries suited to less dangerous times.

If you didn't work, what could you possibly do with yourself? In the days immediately following my resignation from Chevrolet-Indianapolis, the sentence from the GM pamphlet haunted me: I slept later and later each morning, I watched television, I made telephone calls, I wandered around The Meadows Shopping Center, I wrote a few letters to friends telling them I'd quit my job, and, as before, I bided my time, waiting for the weekends.

An editor at a New York publishing house wrote to say she was holding the manuscript of my last novel (which she thought publishable) during a turnover in company management; she was hoping that the incoming editorial board would be more receptive to new fiction— and so I watched the mailbox daily for good news, but none came.

Within a month—by the second or third week in January (1961)—I was writing again, working not on a novel, but on a long letter to the new President, a letter which I conceived of as being the basis for a political campaign which would be national in scope, international in effect. I worked on the letter every day, all day—and at the end of January I moved out of The Meadows and back to Bloomington—to be near Ginny, to continue revising the letter, perfecting my campaign.

When the letter was finished, my campaign would begin; I would send copies of the letter to every major newspaper, magazine, TV station, radio station, and public official in America. Once the letter was publicized, Kennedy would be pressured to answer it publicly. Since my conclusions followed directly from his assumptions, he would either have to acknowledge the validity of my position—or evade my questions. In either case, the furor surrounding my letter would arouse young men all around the country to refuse—in massive numbers—to serve in the military.

This plan had had one earlier counterpart. My first novel (*Joel Campus: College Prophet*), written when I was a sophomore at Columbia, had told the tale of a college student, who, believing he is about to die, has a visionary experience. He delivers his vision—his "message" —to the mass media, they publicize it, he becomes a national hero, the center of a new cult, the savior of millions. I was aware of the parallels between what I had written and what I was doing; the novel, however, had been a satire. It had made fun of America's penchant for heroes, messages, messiahs. It seemed impossible that I could ever be as ridiculous as the hero of my first novel had been. The novel ended, the first time around, with the hero discovering that he is not, in fact, going to die, and that his message, therefore, is without basis; thus, he must invent a way of committing suicide which will sustain his myth and the actual good it has done. In the second version of the novel, written during my senior year at Columbia, the hero jumps off a cliff.

I had made my own decision to apply for C. O. status shortly before I'd left GM. By the time I arrived in Bloomington I was equipped with an arsenal of pacifist arguments. I was in possession of the *Handbook for Conscientious Objectors*, and I could defend my position on moral, practical, historical, and religious grounds. I could point out, for example, the distinction between personal violence and organized violence, thus retaining the right to defend my wife and grandmother against armed rapists. The central fact remained nuclear: the possibility that any war could now become the last war was all important. While I might admit, in arguments, that nonnuclear war was sometimes justified if it defended men against some absolute evil (Hitler, Nazism), I would never admit that nuclear war was justified in the defense of relative goods against relative evils.

Most important: all human beings, like all Organization Men, had the right (the moral obligation) to say No to something if they believed saying No was right. I could best serve my country and mankind by trying to stop it from continuing in its madness. When I doubted my own arguments, though, I was reinforced by something new—by the knowledge that I could not be part of any Army. Although I had never applied for a deferment and still felt loyal to the American GI's who, in the schoolyard legends of my youth, had saved me from becoming a lampshade for Hitler, I now felt, without even seeking out the reason, though I remembered that, to my great unhappiness, my mother had forbade me to play with guns when I was a boy, that if I were drafted and if somebody were to put a gun into my hands, I would have smashed it to bits.

At the time, my campaign did not seem strange or grandiose, total success did not seem impossible. Once I'd decided that I wouldn't serve, and once I'd envisioned the consequences (I'd go to jail?—All right then, I'd go to jail), the Kantian imperative, strong in me always, went to work. My decision to refuse military service was too important to be left personal, to be wasted on my individual and unpublicized life.

A year before, Norman Mailer had begun *Advertisements for Myself* with the following observation: "Like many another vain, empty, and bullying body of our

time, I have been running for President these last ten
years in the privacy of my mind. . . ." In the privacy of
my own mind, the presidency was merely an office whose
influence I had to make use of in order to save all mankind.

I took passages from Kennedy's inaugural address—
questioned them, analyzed them, refuted them. When
Kennedy spoke about a torch which had been "passed to
a new generation of Americans," I noted that I was "of
another generation, also born in this century, but knowing little of the actuality of war, knowing much more
about the legacy of the last war. . . . As a member of a
different and newer generation I see one paramount
objective: the removal of the threat to existence. . . ."

The letter went on like this for six typewritten pages
and it repeated, often, the fact that the next world war
would be the last one. Under the aspect of this eternity,
all ordinary considerations faded: "It is not just a question of being freer than other societies, or defending my
own particular nation," I wrote at the end. "Such realities
are relative realities. War will be absolute—the absolute
annihilation of life . . .

> I speak only for myself in this letter, and I hope that
> you will consider it carefully. I would also hope for some
> answer—considering my position and the questions I
> have raised, what do you advise me? and why and for
> what? If I am blind to some considerations larger than
> any touched on, what are they? Can I, with "good con-
> science" and with "history the final judge" of my deeds
> —can I give my personal commitment to any war or de-
> fense effort?

The depression which had enveloped me at GM was
suddenly gone—in fact, while I worked on the letter, inquired about mimeograph machines, made lists of news-

papers and politicians, TV stations and magazines, I was happier than I'd been in a long time—happy, in fact, in the way I'm happy only when the first draft of a novel is going well. (The slightly high feeling I experienced in the midst of working on the letter would return, in the years after this, whenever I plunged into political activity— feeling, always, despite what I knew, that what I was doing had a chance to actually change things. Even now, it seems, almost ten years after GM, I still throw myself into political activities and battles with the same energy and expectations that are with me when I work on a novel—i.e., with the feeling that when I am done some- thing new will exist, something which had no existence before I helped give it existence. Though I like to think I do whatever I do without illusion, and without the naïve and laughable fury which drove me in the months after GM, I have not, after all, as even this narrative proves, changed so much.)

When the letter was in its next-to-final form and my plans had evolved, I felt sure enough of myself to be poli- tic, to compromise. "It was not until almost a month after his inauguration that I finished the letter," I would write later that spring, accurately reflecting my state of mind at the time. "By then I had decided to send the letter—at least at first—only to President Kennedy, giving him the courtesy of a reply before I initiated any kind of crusade."

One thing did puzzle me, but only slightly: none of my friends seemed convinced that my letter would do what I said it would, or even get to Kennedy's desk ("But don't you see," I'd point out, "if it appears concurrently as an open letter in hundreds of newspapers and magazines, he'll have to answer it—!") Ginny, Arnie, other graduate students I showed drafts of the letter to—they were all skeptical, unenthusiastic, patronizing.

I had not, obviously, explained myself fully or clearly

enough—for if I had, I was certain, everybody would have agreed with me. So I pressed on, day after day, searching for the precise phrasing, the key fact, the logic that would do nothing less than make everything clear to everybody.

The first week in February I received a "Current Information Questionnaire" from my local draft board. It was the first correspondence I'd had with them since I'd registered at eighteen, almost five years before, and it seemed a real enough reason to abandon work on the letter. Such questionnaires normally preceded, by several months, notices for physicals, and the physicals preceded induction.

Conscientious objection and jail, war and the military—such things were suddenly less abstract. When Arnie and another friend offered me a ride back to New York during intersession, I packed my things and said good-bye to Ginny. I was let off under an elevated subway line somewhere in the Jamaica section of Queens. I put my luggage into a taxi and arrived at my parents' apartment in Flushing (they had moved there during my senior year at Columbia) past midnight, waking them. I had not told them I was coming home.

I greeted my father with the news that he would, at last, be proud of me—I had finally become "politically concerned." Though I did no more work on the letter or the campaign after I arrived home, I did show the letter to my father, informing him of my plans for a national crusade.

He screamed. His temper, equal to my passion, made us incapable of sustaining a discussion on the letter, or on my new political views for five minutes before he was in a rage which made my mother rush to calm us both down. He seemed to interpret my attacks on America as attacks on him, though I professed at the time to find the analogy absurd.

"I *love* America!" I remember him screaming several times, veins showing in his neck, his body shaking with anger. And with this sentence all arguments were included, all arguments came to an end.

My parents were, by turns, angry, concerned, worried. With my "mind," and education I could have been "anything"—a professor, an executive—"anything at all." Instead, I slept late, I talked of being a novelist, I involved myself in "mishugenah" fantasies. But I was, at last, if only in the four and a half small rooms of a Flushing apartment, *important.* My letter had the power to evoke from my mother and father what it evoked from no one else in the world—strong emotional reactions, and these soothed my deepest fears.

A few weeks at home, a few battles with my parents —these quickly destroyed whatever desire remained to work on the letter. What I dared not admit at the time was, in effect, true: that they had the power—from the anger and worry I induced in them I could believe that it was I who had power over them—to stop me from sending the letter.

I answered the "Current Information Questionnaire" and sent it back to my draft board. My feelings concerning Conscientious Objection remained firm, and I discussed these, too, with my parents, with friends. Without the letter to Kennedy attached, I found that people were more direct with me. In general, they voiced respect for my beliefs, for my courage, though I had, as yet, risked nothing except words—but they went on to conjure up the trouble my beliefs would create for me: I would not be able to get jobs, I would be involved in legal hassles, I would go to jail. The easiest, and therefore the best, thing to do was either to accept induction and try to get a desk

job, to find an opening in a six-month National Guard
Unit, or to get a deferment by going back to graduate
school.

I was determined to avoid all three possibilities. I
had long discussions with friends who were in my
position—unmarried, in their early twenties, eligible for
induction—and my own solution, to apply for alternative
service as a C. O., began to seem less eccentric. One high
school and college friend, Arthur Rudy, in training in
clinical psychology at the time, made me one of his first
nonpaying patients. Whether we talked on the phone,
during walks along Flatbush Avenue, or sitting against
the fence in a schoolyard between games of three-man
basketball, I was able to test my thoughts, my plans, un-
sure, half-formed, "different," in discussions, arguments
with him. "Noogie, be realistic—" was a standard response on his part—an introduction to a way of seeing
what I was doing which allowed me, afterwards, to be
just that: realistic. "The Noog in jail? What good would
that do—?" (Five years later, when he was part of an
Army medical team stationed in a village hospital in Vietnam, his wife and one-year-old daughter left behind in
America, he would offer—without my asking—to write a
letter in support of the C. O. application I was at last, at
twenty-seven, filing.)

Once I had accepted the fact of my impotence when
it came to single-handedly bringing about world disarmament, I could also accept a return to the writing of fiction. I began a new novel, its setting (strangely enough)
at an automobile plant in a conservative Midwest city. I
waited each morning until my parents were gone to
work, then got out of bed, went downstairs for the *Times*,
returned, ate breakfast, began work. Robert was living in
Manhattan at the time, and I had the apartment to myself; my desk, tucked now in the corner of an eight-by-

ten-foot bedroom, was the old kitchen table from Brooklyn.

I established a routine: writing in the mornings,
playing ball and visiting neighborhood bars in the afternoons, leaving the house before my parents returned from
work, spending the evenings with girls, with friends,
drinking. The writing didn't go well. It went more slowly,
in fact, than first-draft writing had ever gone for me. The
problem, I realized after a month or so, was that the emotions which had been with me during the preceding
months were still sloshing around inside, and they threatened, I feared, to turn my novel into an allegorical ren-
dering of the letter to Kennedy.

If, a few months before, I'd had to do away with my
desire to write fiction in order to be political, now, I felt,
I had to do away with my desire to be political in order
to be a novelist. I settled on a plan: I would write an
essay about the letter, and about what (at GM) had generated it, thus exorcising the political emotions.

I put the novel aside (I knew already that it would
concern a 1955 wildcat strike—and that this strike would
be set against a background of the workers' memories of
real strikes from the early days of union organizing) and
began the essay. The essay grew. Before long it was concerning itself less and less with what, in my GM experience, had brought me to write the letter. It became, increasingly, section by section, a detailed explication and
proof—a justification *of* the letter, a book—one which
was, in brief, a polemic against war, racism, industrialism,
militarism, capitalism, totalitarianism, imperialism, and
inertia.

On the title page I placed, as an epigraph, Newton's
first law: "Every body persists in a state of rest or of uni-
form motion in a straight line unless compelled by external force to change that state."

I reprinted the letter to Kennedy in the first chapter
—and discovered that I still believed in it. If only others
could be made to see the truth of what I had seen, then
perhaps there was still hope. To give body to my arguments I read everything I could on the arms race, on civil
rights—I visited the offices of SANE, of civil rights groups
—and my researches confirmed the worst fears I had carried with me from Indiana: America was deeply and fun-
damentally conservative, the arms race would inevitably
kill us all, men were not free.

The process of writing the book, however—despite
my apocalyptic prophecies—seemed to remove most of
my own fears. Having to write about what I thought had
caused me to write the letter seemed to free me from
those very things. The generalizations I put forward
about the world invariably described my own state; and
the way in which I described fear as being at the center
of things was a just (though, at the time, unacknowl-
edged) description of my own condition. Though my in-
sights were neither very new nor very precise, I wrote my
way to them as if nobody before me had ever experienced
them. In my abstracted condition—as I relived my eight
months in Indianapolis—real things seemed to dissolve,
and it was the very *in*substantiality of the enemy which
became his secret and most terrible weapon. Thus, I concluded a long analytic discussion of the causes of the
world's ills by revealing my discovery that fear "coerces,
controls, destroys, dictates, and enslaves more powerfully
when it is the result of an invisible force."

Although my resistance movement included only
myself, my prose carried me away and within three
months the book was finished. It ended with a call for
massive resistance to the military—and every sentence of
it was written in a style which, when I'd look through the
book in the years since, would always cause the same re-

action: My God—did I really write this? (I liked to think I'd outgrown this style, but often, noticing the capsule sermons which would materialize mysteriously on pages I'd written, I'd have to wonder.) I took on the voice of one who spoke for my generation, and I ended with a flourish, feeling I had found a genuinely new voice, unaware of how closely my rhetoric resembled the President's, of how much it resembled the speeches in the "I Speak For Democracy" contests of my grade-school days:

> And if I presume to speak not only for myself, but for other young people with similar doubts and emotions and fears and hopes and faiths, let me say that we know these things:
>
> We know that in this nuclear age, where war will mean killing civilians en masse, where biological and chemical and radiation warfare may already be more advanced than killing by bombs, in this age we cannot give our commitment blindly. We will not let others do our thinking for us. We must ask questions and be answered. We know that the problems are difficult and that there are no sure or easy answers. But we also know that the present methods of dealing with reality seem worse than useless—they seem hopeless. We will not aid in the destruction of man. Hard work must be done if we want to survive, if we want to enjoy peace and freedom. We will gladly help in that work.

My fourth book was done (I was twenty-three), and I brought it to the SANE office, where the National Director read it, praised it, and sent me to Norman Cousins. Cousins was then Honorary Chairman of SANE, and editor-in-chief of the *Saturday Review*. I had relied, for some of my information, on his book, *In Place of Folly*, and to have a direct introduction to him made me feel that I was getting somewhere.

I did not, in fact, ever see him or hear from him. A

month later, the editorial assistant who had taken the manuscript from me, returned it, telling me that it was "the most incredible piece of political writing" by a young man that she had ever read. She was probably right.

I returned home and the next day I was back at work on my novel; I had dealt—in a tangible way—with the guilt that bound my fiction to my politics. The political book was there; in fact, by having turned my political emotions into a book, I had made them into something that was doubtless more real to me than anything else could have been. While I waited to hear from *Saturday Review* or any of the other magazines and publishers I would submit it to, I could justify what I felt a need to justify (would always feel a need to justify)—the fact that I was no longer working full time to save mankind.

I had, I even began to see, been somewhat excessive in my politics—perhaps, I admitted, even slightly paranoid. Certainly I had been unrealistic. Now, however, things were different—I was writing again, I was away from Indiana, from The Meadows, from General Motors. The letter to Kennedy had been a silly, misconceived scheme, and I was, I would tell friends, embarrassed by the fact that I could have gotten so insanely involved in it, in the idea of the campaign which would surround it.

My new manuscript, on the other hand, I would point out, once it was published as a book, would be able to do what I as an individual, and what the letter alone, could never have done.

This new, more "realistic" view of things had other effects. Although I felt more certain than ever that I would have chosen jail before military service, I now saw no reason for precipitating the need for such a choice. The practical thing to do was to use the freedom I had in order to work for the policies in which I believed—and so

I became involved in my first actual political activities.

There were, in New York, people who were fighting the same enemies I had been fighting, and this now seemed to me a reassuring fact. If those who had already risked their jobs and lives, as many in the civil rights movement had done, could continue to do so—and could continue to commit their time and energies to mundane tasks which didn't seem to promise any imminent apocalypse, who was I, who had done nothing but write down my feelings, not to join my cause with theirs? The isolation in which I'd been living became less necessary; it had already become less pleasurable.

I began, then, in whatever time I had left over from writing and in whatever ways were available, to work with whatever particular political group or cause seemed current, just. And the work I did—stuffing envelopes, standing in at UN vigils, collecting clothes for CORE—had its own rewards: for there I was, I could tell myself, the person who had written the book that would electrify and change the nation, the world—and nobody knew it. To those who struggled alongside me, to those who watched me—I was just another ordinary human being, doing my little bit to make the world a better place to live in.

I participated that spring in my first act of civil disobedience. I was on the Columbia campus on a Friday, and was given a handbill announcing a sit-in on the steps of Low Library during the hour when everybody was required by law to take shelter as part of the civil defense program. When the sirens began wailing at noon, I sat down with several hundred other protesters. About fifteen minutes after the drill started two police cars raced across the campus, but they didn't stop, and when the all-clear signal was given forty-five minutes later, we got up and went our separate ways. Nobody was arrested.

Still, the experience was exhilarating. That hundreds

of people would risk jail, would sit silently in moral wit-
ness, would sing together at the end ("We Shall
Overcome")—seemed to me good, noble, thrilling. I was
able, in the flush of having finally "done something," to
strike up a conversation with a girl who had sat near me
during the drill. She wore a peasant's blouse, slipped
down across her shoulders. She had a large mouth, a
straight white smile, long blond hair that spilled down
her back. She smiled at me, and when I looked into her
face her eyes didn't waver—she was, in short, a radical
New York Jewish boy's dream of an Aryan princess: a
blond aristocrat committed to left-wing causes. I was
able, within five minutes, to let her know that I was an
unpublished novelist, that I had already written a political book on massive resistance which was probably going
to be published, that I was on the campus because I was
having drinks later that afternoon at the Faculty Club
with Richard Chase (she was in the Graduate English
Department). She extended her hand. "It's been good
talking with you," she said as we shook hands. "I have to
meet my husband now—he'll be getting out of class . . ."

By the beginning of the summer, my new novel was
past the halfway point, and the money I'd saved at GM
was almost gone. For July and August I took a job helping to run a summer recreation program for muscular
dystrophy children; we took wheelchair patients on outings several times a week (I drove the VW microbus)—to
ball games, parks, movies, Coney Island, Jones Beach,
etc. Since the outings were, most of the time, in the afternoons and evenings, I was able to retain most mornings
for writing.

In my "realistic" frame of mind I also decided to file
an application with the Columbia University Placement
Office. I would become a teacher.

I knew I couldn't leave myself adrift for the fall, dependent on my parents; I knew (said that) it was foolish to think that the next day's mail would bring an acceptance from a publisher of one of my books; I didn't want to return to graduate school, and I went weak at the thought of being drafted. Teaching would give me money, a deferment, and time for writing. I would be finished by three o'clock every day; I would have summers and vacations free.

In late June I flew out to Indiana. As I suppose I'd known when I'd left Bloomington, things had gone bad—in letters, phone calls—with Ginny, and, suddenly realizing I would lose her, I discovered I didn't want to. I stayed in Bloomington for a week. I brought my new manuscripts with me (the political book, half of the automobile plant novel) and Ginny read them, but she didn't —as with other things—have much to say. This hurt most of all. I tried to get her to comment on various sections, ideas, characters—but she let me know that if she did, I would feel even worse than I was feeling, something which hardly seemed possible.

At the end of the summer, she came to New York for job interviews, and we met twice. By this time I'd accepted a position at a private school in Saddle River, New Jersey, and things seemed to be going well: I was involved with several girls (my political activities had led me to places where I'd discovered relatives of the girl I'd met on the steps of Low Library), the first draft of the novel was almost done. Still, when we said good-bye for the last time—we'd gone together for almost two years—I felt shattered, drained.

I felt, in fact, almost exactly the way I'd felt during my last month at Chevrolet-Indianapolis. I was unable to do any writing, I talked to myself, I felt sorry for myself, trapped. The week in which we met for the last time was the week I moved to Saddle River.

The school was set on a beautifully landscaped estate

of several hundred acres, and the headmaster gave me a rent-free room in back of the school in what had been, previously, the servants quarters. Outwardly, as at GM, I must have seemed happy, assured, untroubled. The school, in its second year of existence, had less than a hundred students, from fourth to twelfth grade, and the atmosphere was peaceful, intimate, friendly. I got along well with my students, the other teachers, and with the headmaster, despite the fact that he called me into his office during the first week of classes to "recommend" that I not wear plaid shirts with ties.

When the school emptied each day, and the headmaster had gone home, I remained on the estate, sharing it with one other person—the gardener. His name was Stiney, and according to the deed, whoever bought the property had to agree to take care of him, to let him stay on as gardener. He was in his fifties, wore his hair to his shoulders, tied Indian-style, his shirt was open to the waist, and he spoke with birds and animals. He was a strict vegetarian, and a suspicious one: he refused to allow anyone in the school to give him food, or to fix his meals for him. The FBI, he told me, was sending agents into Saddle River to kill him. In his room, down the hall from mine, he kept stones on top of all the electrical wires to stop the electricity from jumping out when it had to turn corners. In his closet he had jars of alcohol which prevented lightning from coming down the chimneys and setting the school on fire.

He kept several trunks in his room; they were locked and I became one of the few people ever to see their contents. They were filled with rocks, and the cracks on the rocks represented, if I understood him correctly, maps of various countries in the world; the maps possessed magical properties and Stiney, by interpreting them, was able to predict the future.

Sometimes he would visit my room at night to tell

me stories, most of which I couldn't follow. He often spent his afternoons changing his money from bank to bank, and the reasons for this, which he explained at length to me, involved secret cameras, FBI agents, the Russian government, Indians, the harmful effects of eating meat, and—I could only nod my head—the invention of the automobile. We shared the upstairs servants quarters for several weeks (our rooms were about ten feet apart and the lock on my door was broken), and, when the estate was deserted at night, despite the fact that he trusted me, I had a hard time falling asleep—I thought of my writing, my books, Ginny, the school, my future, and, most of all, I wondered if I would wake in time on the night that Stiney slipped down the corridor, his hair flowing, his chest bare, a rock in his hand.

The headmaster gave me the school limousine, a 1941 Chrysler nine-seater, to use until I bought my own car, and on my way to New York one weekend, just before I reached the George Washington Bridge, it broke down. I had it towed into a repair shop, where, when I stepped on the accelerator, the oil tank exploded, nearly killing the three mechanics whose heads were looking in under the hood. I trembled all weekend.

Though I was able to get through each day of teaching—I helped coach the football team in the afternoons, and enjoyed this—though I seemed to be functioning in a real world, my spirits were lower than ever and my novel remained unfinished. Once again, as at GM, I projected each day of work twenty and thirty years ahead. I would, I became convinced, be an unmarried teacher in a rich man's school, correcting grammar exercises nightly, for the rest of my life.

That I got on easily, successfully with my students— more easily than with people my own age; that some of my students were the same age as girls I saw on weekends—such things confused me. I waited (again, as at GM) for the weekends, but they were no help. I found, when I drove on highways and country roads, that I was now playing games: not pulling to the side of the road when tears, there for no apparent reason, would blind me so that I couldn't see where I was going; veering from lane to lane; seeing how long I dared drive without touching the steering wheel. Robert outdid me, though: he came to New Jersey several times to spend weekends with me, and during one, while we were driving from Saddle River to Teaneck along Route 4 late at night, he suddenly swung open the door of the car and threatened to jump.

FIVE: *Pictures from an Institution*

For cooping up all these lunatics in this old clois-
ter becomes, I think, a dangerous thing, in which
you risk losing the little good sense that you may
still have kept. Not that I am set on this or that by
preference. I am used to the life here, but one
must not forget to make a little trial of the opposite.

—*Vincent Van Gogh,* in a letter to his brother,
Theo. December 31, 1889.

Near the end of my second month at Saddle River,
after eating supper with Stiney in the school kitchen
one night, I went upstairs to my room, took my typewriter
from my closet, and carried it with me into the classroom
building. I repeated one sentence to myself, again and
again—a sentence from one of my unpublished novels: If
you're a writer, you write; if you don't write, you're not a
writer. In the novel—the one I wrote during the year I
cut graduate-school classes—the sentence is directed at a
forty-year-old professor by his wife. He is in the midst of
a crisis, brought on in part by the fact that he is a famous
critic, a popular teacher, yet still yearns to be a novelist.

At the point in the novel when she says this to him, he has just returned home from a brief and wild affair with a woman he had lived with in his early twenties, when he was trying to write novels. The former girlfriend is now a well-known poet and has been visiting the small New England college where he teaches, in order to give a poetry reading.

I put the lights on in my ninth-grade home room, and waited. At the end of the second hour I began writing, and what I'd taken for the most severe crisis of my life was over—it had, in fact, lasted little more than a month.

I was pleased with what I wrote—a satirical protest against bomb shelters written in the form of a letter from John F. Kennedy's cat. What pleased and relieved me most was that I'd tried to deal humorously with something that I had, until then, been able to regard only with dead seriousness.

I mailed the piece out that week, and it was quickly rejected by several magazines; I was, however, prepared for such an eventuality; a letter involving Kennedy and bomb shelters led directly to the mimeograph machine; making use of the school facilities one night, I ran off several hundred copies of the letter and mailed them to friends, magazines, peace organizations, newspapers, and prominent individuals. One of the peace organizations, The Fellowship of Reconciliation, asked if I would permit them to publish the letter in their magazine, *Fellowship*. I was in possession of my first "acceptance," and I telephoned everybody I knew to tell them so.

I was back at work on the automobile plant novel immediately, and I finished it sometime in November or December and sent it out. By this time I had bought an old 1951 Buick, and had moved from my back room in the school to an apartment in Teaneck, New Jersey.

I had, then, within a year of leaving GM, written two books that derived from my experiences there. More important, I thought, I was—my political activities being the evidence—a totally different person than I'd been when I'd left graduate school in the spring of 1960. That year, and in all the years since, I would seize on the fact of my GM experience as a way of explaining to others why I had (as I thought), suddenly—at the age of twenty-two—changed, become politically radical.

The emotions, feelings, concerns that were aroused during my days at Chevrolet-Indianapolis—these had probably, in some form, been in me before, I'd admit, but it was GM which had caused them to surface. Moreover, I would often claim—as I did in the political book I wrote that year, and as I thought I'd be doing when I began this narrative—almost all the political activities and emotions which have engaged me in the years since have been a working out of what I felt during my half year there, much, I would sometimes note, in the way a novel is the working out, the unwinding of a single vivid feeling or impression—an attempt to recapture and to give narrative life to a single moment.

Things are not—have never been—that simple. Though a brief explanation of the effect my six months at GM had on me often seemed a persuasive enough reason for some changes in me, the explanation always seemed too easy, too neat. Still, even here, I shy away from delving into other, more personal origins for whatever changes I've undergone in the last ten years. I find, though I touch on things in my family, my childhood, that my motivations do not really interest me so much, or rather, that I resist analysis of my motivations. Not only because I rest in this essay on a prejudice (a defense mechanism) which derives from my sense of myself as a novelist—from my feeling that my job as a writer is to de-

scribe action in such a way that motivation is implied—
but from a feeling that whatever motivations a reader
may infer should themselves be permeated with mystery.
My way—inevitably romantic—of defending myself
against the possibility that there may be clear, mechanis-
tic, deterministic, unmysterious, and unambiguous expla-
nations for my actions, my life; that there may not be
some terrible—ultimate—relations between what I am as
a writer and what I am in the rest of my life; that the
sources for both my writing and my actions in the external world may not themselves have sources which are
deep, mysterious, and unknown.

Which is one oblique way of introducing the fact
that, a year after I'd left GM, I was involved in an experience more personal than political—an experience that,
unlike GM, had no discernible (final) beginning or end
point—one which affected those things I call (called) my
political emotions at least as profoundly as assembly lines
did.

Shortly after I'd finished my automobile plant novel
and sent it out, Robert, eighteen years old at the time,
began a journey through the madness of city, private, and
state mental hospitals—a journey which would take several years until, largely through his own courage, his own
humor, he emerged whole, himself at the other end—back
again for better or worse in the "real" world.

His first hospitalization that winter, coming after my
own shaky days that fall—plunged me deeper into the
fears for my own mind and future which had first
plagued me in Indiana. Robert and I had been very close,
and though we had known—had talked for some time
about the possibility of hospitalization, we both fiercely
resisted the thought, fought against the actuality.

The first time I visited him in a city hospital—he was
locked behind iron doors, tied in a straitjacket—though I felt

shattered, defeated, uncertain about everything, the visit
had a stabilizing effect on me. Much as—in my love, my
guilt—I might have wanted to change places with him, to
have taken his place so that he could be set free (wishes I
would voice often in the next few years), I did what I
knew I had to do to make sure that this would not happen. I clung to whatever I felt promised my own self-
preservation.

I did this mostly by transforming his hospitalization
and its effect on me, things I knew were beyond my control, into things abstract—into part of the political field
theory I'd begun developing at GM. What was terrible—
evil—at both GM and mental hospitals, what, that is, destroyed others and could do the same to me, were related, and if I could spell out this relationship, I could, in
my mind, gain control over it. Robert's hospitalization,
then, became the clearest, the final proof—in my emotions
and my theories—of the injustice of things, of the need
for revolution.

The edge of these emotions and theories was rage;
for every sinking, confused feeling in me I compensated
with anger—at the fact that he was imprisoned while
others—less good, less virtuous, less sane, less worthy—
were free; at the inadequacy of the hospitals he was
forced—by himself, by our family, by the world—to be
part of; at my inability to get him out.

The general stupidity and indifference of the world
were evidenced for me in the particular stupidity and indifference of mental hospitals. How, I would demand,
could a human being "get well" when the conditions of
his environment told him—not in words, but in the pris-
on-like architecture, the mammoth dormitories for sleeping, the primitive forms of therapy, the shortage of
trained personnel—that the world didn't really care much
about him. Once, brought back to a state hospital after

what had been diagnosed as an "acute psychotic episode," he was placed in a maximum security ward. A week later we telephoned his doctor to find out how he was doing, only to discover that his doctor had not yet been informed that he was back in the hospital.

One had only to look around and see what society's priorities were: when I looked at the world in those days I saw the ease with which money could be obtained for new highways, for space programs, for new model cars, for marching bands, for advertising—and I needed to see and know no more.

How, I asked at the time, could anyone become "sane" in an institution in which he was surrounded all day by the "insane?" (Robert: "You have to be crazy to want to stay here—" Or, telling me not to worry about him: "I'm sane, don't you see, Jay—? That's what it means to be here—I'm *in* sane.") In my analysis of the situation, I had, I was certain, noticed things that few others had seen. My theory developed: Because of its meager budget and staff, the institution had to place primary emphasis on what were custodial values—i.e., since its burden, day by day, was to try to keep things quiet and orderly, patients who were manic and/or aggressive, for example, were more trouble than patients who were passive and/or depressed, and they were treated accordingly: with security wards, straitjackets, less and less of the already limited, inadequate therapy—and even, at a supposedly decent private hospital, with punishment, confinement to quarters, loss of passes out of the hospital.

In short, the needs of the institution, not of the "patients," seemed to me generally to determine the forms of treatment. And the needs of the institution, I concluded, were determined by the society which created it, funded it, and declared that people placed in it, designated as "mental patients," be, in effect, invalidated as human beings—all rights, decisions, property, etc. taken away from them—so that they could become, in this institutionally mad logic—somehow "human again," "part of society," "responsible for themselves."

In the self-justifying deterministic logic of the hospital, my version of things was not, of course, true: patients, the argument went, always acted so as "to get what they wanted." It followed, therefore, that if patients wound up confined to their rooms, in security wards, without therapists, without doctors—that they must have "wanted" to. °

"The shits," Mailer wrote in *Advertisements for Myself,* "are killing us." The sentence spun around in my head, rested there. The shits, I vowed, would not get me (too). And the shits seemed to me to be everywhere—free, walking the earth, sitting in offices, inflicting suffering, enjoying life while (because) others despaired.

The sight of hundreds of visitors—other brothers, mothers, fathers, friends, relatives—waiting in long lines several times a week, laden with shopping bags and packages, eyes darting with fear, anxiety, anticipation—to spend an hour or two with their beloved inmate, always seemed more terrible to me—obscene was the word I used—than what actually existed behind the locked

---

° Cf. the following account given by Erving Goffman, in *Asylums:* ". . . Persons who are lodged on 'bad' wards find that very little equipment of any kind is given them—clothes may be taken away from them each night, recreational materials may be withheld, and only heavy wooden chairs and benches provided for furniture. Acts of hostility against the institution have to rely on limited, ill-designed devices, such as banging a chair against the floor or striking a sheet of newspaper sharply so as to make an annoying explosive sound. And the more inadequate this equipment is to convey rejection of the hospital, the more the act appears as a psychotic symptom, and the more likely it is that management feels justified in assigning the patient to a bad ward. When a patient finds himself in seclusion, naked and without visible means of expression, he may have to rely on tearing up his mattress, if he can, or writing with faeces on the wall—actions management takes to be in keeping with the kind of person who warrants seclusion."

doors. And the sight of the same people, after visiting hours, waiting in long lines for city buses to take them home, though less overtly terrible, seemed more depressing.

How, I would ask, could anybody place faith in these hospitals, how could anybody place faith in any of the world's institutions, when—in one of the largest hospitals in the most progressive state of the most advanced nation in the civilized world—the Director was still clinging to authoritarian notions in which the hospital was analogous to a church, and, I reasoned at the time, the doctors to priests, the patients to sinners. In what everybody else took for a harmless notice placed on the doors of the hospital—a plea for "appropriate" dress by visitors (no shorts, no low necklines), I was able to see stupidity, insanity, the epitome of all the lies and misconceptions and errors that were responsible for the tragic state of the world. "Although a hospital is not a house of worship," the notice began, "it does partake somewhat of the same solemnity and dignity. . . ." I quenched the fire of my rage by tearing the notice from the door, taking it home with me, brooding over it.

Although I felt I had no choice but to act as if I too had faith in the hospital, the system assigned to "cure" people, my desire again, as at GM, was to destroy: There was more hope in organizing patients (with the support of their aides—almost all black, all underpaid—their doctors, their relatives, their friends) to strike, to picket, to revolt, to blow up the hospitals—than there was in letting things continue as they were.

At one point, on the advice of a friend, a child psychologist at Harlem Hospital, I wrote letters to several private clinics (clinics he said were especially trained to offer my brother the chance he needed), giving my brother's history, inquiring about openings, telling something of our family, of our financial situation. I received replies which thanked me for my "moving letter" but noted that such clinics could "not think" of accepting a patient (there were no "scholarships" one psychiatrist wrote) unless the family of the patient could "guarantee" the doctors for several years, sums which would run, annually between fifteen and twenty-five thousand dollars.

If I'd needed any further evidence for my belief that the inadequacy of mental hospitals was a direct product, a true reflection of our indices of priority, our economic-social-political system, I now had it. True enough, I'd admit at the time, there were people who got well in state hospitals who were not helped in such private clinics, but if one had to "go out of one's mind" for a while, it might be more pleasant to do so in pleasant surroundings: on a beautiful estate, with a private nurse, with good professional care, with daily and individual therapy, etc. At the least, it would be nice if one could enjoy the cures available to others, to the rich, if one could "make a little trial of the opposite."

My life at the Saddle River Country Day School during these months became secondary. I resented the school—the fact that I was part of it—but not with the passion I'd reserved for GM or The Meadows. If the Marxist inside me still insisted on simple dichotomies—the privileged lives the students led did not somehow entitle them to have problems—it didn't stop me from getting to know the students, from liking them. I enjoyed teaching. The students were my daily world and I talked about them with the other teachers endlessly, thought about them always. I seemed to be able to get the students interested in themselves, in their own worlds—and once this was done, they quickly and easily became interested in books, in writing, in new worlds. I brought their once and twice-weekly compositions across the George

Washington Bridge with me on weekends to show friends, and I was, for the better part of my waking hours, respected, admired, even loved; at the time, this was no small thing.

As a teacher, I was able to satisfy my own needs (to be important—the center of attention, the source of change, knowledge), while at the same time satisfying my sense of what a good teacher should be by making my presence, my opinions irrelevant, secondary. The grades I had to put on written work never seemed to affect students adversely—those who had received the lowest grades were as eager (afterwards) to read and show their work as were those who received the highest. On the first day of school, not knowing what to do, I'd assigned "How I Spent My Summer Vacation" as the topic for the first composition in my eighth-grade class. As soon as I heard the students groan, I added, as an afterthought; "And you don't have to tell the truth—" It was the first of my attempts to reverse the conventional—barely original, but it seemed to be enough to set the students free, to set me free, to set the tone for the year.

At the school itself, not wanting, I suppose, to endanger the respect and popularity I'd achieved, I kept my political emotions and theories to myself. In the course of the year I can recall only two things I did which could in any way have been considered political. 1) I refused to make my students take part in civil defense drills in which they would protect themselves from nuclear warheads by crouching under their desks; and 2) I taught *The Catcher In the Rye* despite warnings from the headmaster and his request that I choose another novel. In addition—the events rest in my memory precisely because they were so absurdly minor, so earnestly proletarian—I actually said to a student, with others present, when he came in one day bemoaning the $50,000 his father had lost in a stock market slide the previous day: "Have you ever considered that your father earns money for which he doesn't work?"—and I rooted for an opposing football team (an orphanage) against my own.

I did no writing all winter, but that spring I started and completed two projects. The first was an attempt at a children's book. The teacher with whom I was friendliest at the school was Mrs. Gladys Matthews, and she was in her early eighties at the time. Born and raised in Texas, she was a member of the DAR, the Colonial Dames of America, a descendant of Pocahontas, and had been a staunch supporter of Norman Thomas in the thirties. When she read articles and stories in magazines, she would systematically tear out all the full pages of advertising, muttering as explanation: "I didn't pay for this—" Mrs. Matthews had taught Mexican children in Texas border schools, and one of them had given her the memoirs of an ancestor of his—a guide named Poli (José Policarpo Rodriguez)—famous in Texas during the nineteenth century for having blazed many of its important trails and for having been keeper of the camels when Jefferson Davis had brought them to America just before the Civil War.

"Here you are," she said to me one night, handing me several boxes of yellow-edged pages. "I tried to write a book once and found out I wasn't a writer. So I stopped. I've been waiting thirty years to find somebody to finish the job."

The fact that Poli had lived through both the Mexican and Civil wars without taking part in either intrigued the pacifist-propagandist in me, and I worked on the book every night for several months. The result, however (my fifth complete book), was dismal, and working on it depressed me, only made me aware of the original fiction I was not writing.

The second piece of writing I did that spring was also derivative. By then my political book (*A Letter to Kennedy*) had been rejected by enough publishers to convince me that it would not be published. Several publishers had helped sharpen my sense of injustice (helplessness) by noting that for such a letter to have "relevance," it would have to have been written by "a well-known political figure." Hadn't, I screamed silently, that been the point of the book—that I was *not* well known, that I had not, until GM, been political? I took up such points, at length, in the new article, quoting from my rejection slips, telling the story of the letter, of the book about the letter, of the article about the book about the letter.

I dreaded the idea of a second year as tutor to the rich. I wanted, again, to get far away from New York, from my family. In late spring I applied to the Indiana University School of Letters for the summer session. If I survived it, I decided, I would stay on for the fall and finish my Master's Degree.

The eight weeks in Bloomington were a joy: I played tennis every day, basketball, made good friends with other graduate students, had time for reading, writing, and—what seemed suddenly all important—more than enough of the company, the conversation—about literature, politics, Indiana—I had obviously been hungering for. Having been away from graduate school for two years, having broken the usual pattern—straight from four years of undergraduate studies to graduate school to college-teaching position—I found that I could more easily accept what had previously seemed unacceptable. I was wary, though, fearful—especially about what discussions, papers, theorizing on other novels—when I, at twenty-four, had had none published—would do to me, to my writing.

The world of the university, upon my return to it,

did not impress me as being any more moral in its internal politics, its bureaucracy, its contracts, its own caste system, than GM; still, I discovered, I preferred the business of education to the business of business.

I was struck also by the ways in which the lives of the graduate students impressed me, initially, as being similar to the lives of mental patients. Again, I worked out a theory: graduate students, like mental patients, were protected, insulated from the outside world; they were given fixed rewards and punishments for obeying and disobeying rules; they were taken care of with respect to the necessities of life; they had their own therapists (teachers, advisers, counselors). Undergraduates at the university had always referred to the graduate center as "the zoo"—and I now found the word appropriate; the numbers of graduate students who seemed to me to be misfits, who would not, I felt, have been able to survive in any other environment was astonishing. More than this, it was their physical bearing which had first elicited my reactions, comparisons: stiff neck and shoulders, drugged look about the eyes, tight mouthlines, inability to laugh naturally . . .

Still, I was happier on the campus, among them, than I'd been at GM, at home, or at Saddle River. The pressures within university walls seemed infinitely less severe than those outside it; I had forgotten about the incredible amounts of sheer time a student had to himself and I found, at the end of eight weeks, that I wanted to stay. Even the fact that many of the people I was surrounded by were timid, tight, vulnerable, or strange, came, by this time, to represent something positive for me—i.e., I interpreted their (projected) inability to get on in the outside world as an instinctive rejection of it.

At the end of the summer I sent a letter to the headmaster of the Saddle River Country Day School from Los

Angeles (I'd driven there with some graduate students), telling him of my decision to return to graduate school. I flew to New York after two weeks in California, settled things there, and drove back to Bloomington, where I took an apartment a few blocks from the campus with two graduate students in botany.

Shortly after classes began I repeated, briefly, the games of the previous year: I'd walk the town streets at night and wait until the last second before racing across the paths of oncoming cars. Thanks to the summer tennis and basketball my timing was good—despite blaring horns, screeches, skidding runs, I was never hurt badly. The games lasted for a week or two and never returned.

I received an assistantship in the English Department that fall and I thrived on the teaching. That my freshmen students seemed, in general, inferior to most of my ninth- and tenth-grade students at Saddle River only gave me more reason to assume antic dispositions, to work hard.

Once I asked my classes for a definition of "empiricism." They had just read Bertrand Russell's essay, "Empiricism and Democracy," and I said that I wanted to know how much background I'd need to give them when we discussed the essay during the next class meeting. They should not put their names on their papers, they should not answer if they hadn't had time to read the essay. The word, which appeared not only in the title, but in virtually every paragraph of the essay, was taken by all but two of fifty students to be "a form of government like communism or colonialism."

During my second or third week of teaching we read an essay by Wright Morris, "Abuse of the Past: Norman Rockwell." In the essay, Morris repeatedly uses Rockwell's drawings to illustrate what he describes as the American ability to make of all things "a joke," of the

American inability to face reality—try to imagine a Rockwell drawing of a concentration camp, a bad train crash. I was almost through the class period before I realized that the reason things were not going well was that we were operating on different spectrums; my students, I discovered by a few quick questions, had assumed that Morris was praising Rockwell for his truthfulness. If you couldn't say something good about somebody, they seemed to believe, you shouldn't say anything. I was, I realized, back in the provinces—and I discovered that I didn't mind.

At the end of the second semester my students wrote, without exception, that the value of their year at Indiana, the purpose of their college education, was "to get to know different kinds of people better." That they could not write sentences in English, that any single composition seemed to contain (like the notice on the New York State Hospital door) all the logical, ideological, and philosophical errors of Western Civilization, that they were fundamentalist-conservatives politically (the first essay I looked at the second semester was entitled: "How Franklin Roosevelt Caused the Second World War in Order to Aid International Communism"), that most of them found the classroom an obvious intrusion on the other activities associated with college live (in their lives, the work-pleasure split was natural and untroubled)—I found that I did not become enraged with them for such things. Their prejudice, like their ignorance, seemed profound—in the simplest, most literal way, I said, they didn't know any better.

About a month after classes began—on October 24, 1962, two days after Kennedy announced the Cuban blockade—the campus had its first political demonstration of the year, and I welcomed it, found that I was excited by the possibility that I might be part of it, that I might apply—in some visible way—the experience, knowledge, theories, and emotions that I'd gained since the last time I'd been on the campus.

As soon as an Ad Hoc Committee of students issued a statement calling for a demonstration protesting the blockade, the University administration responded as I knew it would. The Dean of Students, Robert H. Shaffer, issued a statement in which he declared that "Indiana University has always supported the right of the individual student to express himself freely on any political or social issue. We shall continue to support this policy of free expression. . . ." He added, however, that "common sense would suggest that students who consider participation in any public demonstration would understand with whom they are aligning themselves. . . . I am certain that the vast majority of the students will ignore the action of such a small number of students endeavoring to attract attention to themselves." The president of the university, former Secretary of the Army, Elvis J. Stahr, Jr., stated that "the most effective way to deal with minorities with whom *we* disagree in the present kind of situation is to ignore them completely" (italics mine).

I arrived at the University auditorium on the afternoon of October 24 prepared to join the Ad Hoc group as soon as it issued its statement on the crisis. I never got a chance. The several thousand students who were gathered in the square in front of the auditorium hissed, booed, shoved, punched, kicked. The fifteen demonstrators, unable to give their statement, began moving away from the auditorium, and the students followed them.

The day had already been turned into a joke; the protest was another football rally: students carried placards bearing signs such as "Block that Ship!"—a refrain

they chanted again and again. One fraternity paraded
with a sign that stated: "We Believe in Mom's Cherry Pie
and Sex."

Groups of students formed barricades, arms linked,
and kicked and punched the protesters at various points
along the route of their march. The police, who followed
the students across campus, did nothing. When a clergy-
man (the Reverend Paul Killinger, Unitarian minister in
Bloomington) asked one of the policemen why he was
doing nothing to protect the fifteen students, the policeman smiled, and replied that he was only there "to protect the liberties of Americans."

The saddest part of the day concerned the attack on a
young faculty member—a visiting professor from Spain. He
told me afterwards that when he had seen the announcement of the demonstration in the student paper, he had
been thrilled—for the first time since he'd come to America, he was actually going to see how our democracy
worked, how we allowed free speech even in time of crisis. When he saw what actually happened, though, he
suddenly found himself trying to address the crowd,
trying to get them to give the protesters a hearing, to let
them make their statement.

The crowd pressed in on him, he was thrown against
a car, hurled to the ground, punched, kicked. A graduate
student I knew ran to a policeman to tell him that the
professor was being beaten, but the policeman told my
friend, "He shouldn't be here." "It serves him right," said
another.

A week later, still badly cut and bruised, the professor
showed me a letter he had received from the student body
president, Mike Donovan. Donovan had issued a statement after the demonstration, beginning: "This afternoon
the students of Indiana University clearly illustrated one
of the things President Kennedy and the American peo-

ple wish to preserve in this country . . . freedom of speech and the right to dissent. . . ." In his letter to the professor, Donovan said that he had heard about the "alleged" attack on him, but he wanted to remind the professor that "as an alien," he was not, of course, "entitled to the same rights as American citizens. . . ." Donovan was considered the campus "liberal"; the campus "conservative," who received the university's highest award at graduation that June, went on to become the national chairman of the Young Americans for Freedom.

The enemies I'd found in Indianapolis were living in Bloomington also, and I was ready to do more than battle them silently. The day of the demonstrations I was at work on an article and on letters to the student paper, to university officials. The day after the demonstration the student paper made no mention of violence, and though many faculty members and students sent letters about what had happened, the paper, under the direction of the Department of Journalism, refused to print any of them. They refused also to give any reason for their decision, though they did admit to me, on the phone, that they were "acting under orders."

I sent the article out and it was quickly turned down by several national magazines; when, a few months later, the local county prosecutor, Thomas A. Hoadley, brought an injunction against three of the demonstrators, officers of the Young Socialists Alliance, for violating a 1951 Indiana Anti-Communism Statute ("It shall be the purpose of the state of Indiana and the people of Indiana to exterminate Communism and Communists, and any or all teachings of the same. . . ."), I revised the article, sent it to *The Minority of One*, and soon had my second acceptance. (Later that year, when events proliferated, I would write a third article, one which was published in *The New Republic*.)

The sequence of events began to resemble something from *Babbitt*. To "clear the way" for a Grand Jury investigation of the "possible involvement" of the YSA in the demonstration of October 24, the young prosecutor dismissed charges against two nonstudents involved. "The important thing, in this case," he told the press, "is to get this organization off the campus." He announced that he would consider the constitutionality of the YSA (under the 1951 statute), that he would take the case to the Supreme Court "if necessary," and that the action would "definitely not be taken as a witch hunt."

A local grand jury indicted the three officers, but miraculously, the indictment made no mention of the events of October 24—instead it charged the officers with being present at a meeting in which the national secretary of the YSA, Leroy McCrae, had stated that nonviolence might not be the only way for black people to secure political power in places such as Mississippi. The meeting had been held after Hoadley had announced that he would seek to indict the three officers.

Hoadley called the grand jury "courageous," and told the press that "we want only to stamp out Communism and what it stands for before it gets a foothold here." Then he added that because the grand jury could not obtain a list of YSA members, he had not been able to cross-check their names against a list of names compiled in his own narcotics investigation "to determine to what extent, if any, marijuana is used to recruit new members in the YSA." When the indictment was returned, the student senate of I. U. called a special session and went on record—there was one abstention, by a foreign student—as being unanimously "opposed" to the "socialist minority" which was bringing their university into disrepute.

Invited to contribute a guest editorial on the controversy to the local newspaper, *The Bloomington Herald-*

Telephone, Hoadley chose "academic freedom" as his subject. When several faculty members wrote to the paper to point out that fourteen of Hoadley's seventeen paragraphs were lifted verbatim from a famous A. O. Lovejoy speech on academic freedom, Hoadley replied that the Lovejoy speech was more than twenty-eight years old and therefore in the public domain. He added that he had not used quotation marks around Lovejoy's words because he did not want "to impress the university community with [his] literary ability."

Hoadley was a rather bungling parody of a Midwest anti-Communist, but what he was a parody of still seemed to me to be the strongest political strain in the central regions of America. The attitudes exemplified by Hoadley, the police, Donovan, the 1951 Statute, the student senate, the grand jury—these were, I continued to believe, the attitudes held by the majority of Hoosiers, and, I inferred (remembering my eight months in Indianapolis), the majority of Americans.

Those who ended by opposing Hoadley (as Stahr and Shaffer did) were, as they had shown earlier, not really so distant from him. As with the man who had provided the atmosphere for the passing of the 1951 Statute, those who objected to Hoadley did so more because of his "methods" than because of his purpose.

I remember discussing the case with one of the university's best-known professors that spring, a man who considered himself a "liberal." I told him about my articles, my involvement, and he seemed sympathetic. After a while our discussion passed to another I. U. case, that of a journalism professor who had been brought to Indiana to give the Journalism Department prestige and then had been denied tenure because of several articles he'd written for national magazines in which he'd been critical of the university.

The professor agreed with me that a man's opinions outside the classroom should have no effect on his position in the university, that it had probably been a mistake to let this professor go, to in effect, fire him. "Still," he reminded me, "it's a dirty bird who soils its own nest."

If such remarks alienated me from many who styled themselves "liberals," I was no more at home, I found, with the YSA group. Although I did what I could on their behalf, I discovered that their political views impressed me as being enormously deficient in both subtlety and honesty. Most of all, their rhetoric (much of it about The Working Man, the Class Struggle, the Fascist State, etc.) made me twitch. My political reactions remained those of a writer.

I enjoyed being involved in the case; I enjoyed following the day-to-day dramas which attached themselves to events; I enjoyed writing about it, having articles published, getting attention (notoriety) because of my writing (the *Herald-Telephone* announced the publication of my first article on its front page); I enjoyed receiving long letters from people such as Stahr and Shaffer, from professors at other universities who'd been involved in similar episodes. Though I may have found the people in the YSA simplistic and strident—incompatible temperamentally—as long as I could separate myself from them (and from everybody else) by setting my views down on paper and by having those views published, I was willing to work with them, for them. I was, in short, able to do something on a sustained basis about the world which, two years before, had paralyzed me; this pleased me, seemed to help lift me from the fearful melancholy depression of the previous two years. My year in Bloomington was a good one. For better or worse, I realized, things were in proportion: helping three indicted students was not an activity which had much in common with my previous campaigns, but that was all right too.

Early in the year—after a free Friday night showing of Eisenstein's *Alexander Nevsky*—a friend had introduced me to Betsey. She was with him and I was with another girl—but I couldn't, for the rest of the evening, take my eyes from hers. Fortunately—we would laugh about this later, we almost laughed out loud that night— she kept hers on mine. We went out together for the first time a few weeks later—the night, in fact, that I finished my first article on the campus events—and we saw one another every day after that.

In the spring, though, after her mother had undergone open-heart surgery, and my father had suffered several severe coronaries, we decided that it would be best to break up. I'd already accepted a University Fellowship to Columbia for the following fall, which I thought meant —since Betsey had another year to go for her degree at Indiana—that things were bound to end. Better, we both reasoned, sooner than later. Then too, I remembered my father reaching under the plastic oxygen tent to take my hand in his (I'd been summoned to New York when he suffered his second coronary), to ask me to be good to my mother—a request which I interpreted at the time as his dying wish that I never marry a non-Jewish girl.

Still, despite our guilt (Betsey's mother would spell out, in Baptist terminology, the consequences of "living in sin" with a Jew) and our resolutions, we seemed incapable of avoiding each other, we each found ourselves taking strange new routes across campus between classes so that we would—daily and accidentally—meet. And when I finished a piece of writing I found myself doing what I'd done all year—immediately going to see her (telephoning her if she was already locked in her dormitory for the

night) and reading her what I'd written, discussing it
with her.

That winter, in order, I thought, to cheer myself up,
I'd once papered an entire wall of my one-room apartment with rejection slips—and was plunged instanta-
neously into a severe depression which lasted until we'd
both torn down the slips. One Saturday afternoon that
spring, after Betsey and I had "broken up," I returned to
my apartment feeling particularly low, thinking of paper-
ing my wall again. When I unlocked my door, though, I
found Betsey inside, sitting on my bed. "I thought you
might like to play tennis," she said, and smiled.

About a week later she called to tell me that she'd
taken a job in New York for the summer—as waterfront
director at a Girl Scout camp near Port Jefferson, Long
Island. She pointed out that she'd applied for the job before we'd made our decision, and I offered to "show her
around New York" on her days off.

I received my Master's Degree that June and returned to New York, where I rented a single room on the
top floor of a brownstone on West Eighty-fifth Street. In
Columbia's graduate school, I knew, there was no attend-
ance checking, no grades; my fellowship, then, was for
the writing of a new (seventh) book I'd already begun to
pressure-cook. During July and August my writing went
better than it ever had. Betsey came into the city once a
week and I drove out to her camp several times. One
morning, after Betsey had spent the night at my parents'
apartment, I met my father in the kitchen. Nobody else
was awake. He spoke to me in Yiddish and then translated. "From her," he said smiling at me, "you can't get
poisoned." In September, just before she went back to Indiana for her senior year, I asked her to marry me.

That spring and summer, for the first time, I worked
at a new form—the short story—and I discovered that

PICTURES FROM AN INSTITUTION   153

here, too, as in my politics, I was no longer absolute. Most of my work consisted in rejecting ideas, in cutting —i.e., what I left out of a story became as important— more important—than what I included. I no longer seemed to believe that every word or idea or fiction that came from me need save the world, or be saved for it.

In June an editor at a New York publishing house was optimistic about the chances for my automobile plant novel and invited me in to talk about it, asked me if I would be willing to undertake some revisions. What was needed most, we both agreed, was cutting—and when I was done with revisions, a month or two later, we both agreed that the result was immensely superior to the original. Unfortunately, what had been a five-hundred page novel was now a 140-page manuscript.

SIX: *Good-bye to All That*

> Responsible debate and legitimate political action
> —these are the ways to change policies in a demo-
> cratic society. The resisters only retard the cause
> they seem to advance while threatening the foun-
> dation of the freedom they so recklessly exploit.
>
> —editorial, *The New York Times.*

'The only good government,' I said, 'is a bad one
in the hell of a fright; yes, what you want to do
with government is to put a bomb under it every
ten minutes and blow its whiskers off—I mean its
sub-committees. And it doesn't matter if a few of
its legs and arms go too, and it gets blown out of
the window. Not that I've personally got a bad
opinion of governments, as governments. A government is a government, that's all. You don't expect
it to have the virtues of a gorilla because it doesn't
belong to the same class. It's not a higher anthro-
poid. It has too many legs and hands. But if you
blow off some of the old limbs, well, imagine.
There you have a piece of government lying in the
middle of Whitehall, and it says to itself, "This is
most unusual. I distinctly heard a bang. I must en-
quire at once—yes, immediately—I must appoint
a commission." So then it opens its eyes and looks
at the crowd and says, "My God, what has happened, what are these creatures?" And the people
say, "We're the people, you're the government,
hurry up and do something for us." And the gov-

ernment says, "I'll have a committee on it at once."
And the people say, "You haven't got any
committees—they're all dead—you're the government." And the government says, "Haven't I got a
secretary?" And the people shout, "No, we've just
chopped her up with a rusty axe." "Or an office
boy?" "No, we've pushed him down a drain." '

'But I can't be a government all by myself.'

'Yes you are, and you've got to do something.'

'But one man can't be a government, it isn't
democratic.'

'Yes it is,' the people say. 'We've sent for another bomb. But you've got ten minutes still, so
you'd better do something.'

—Joyce Cary. *The Horse's Mouth.*

Encouraged by my first political successes in Indiana—over 100,000 copies of my *New Republic* article
had been reprinted and distributed by the YSA—I returned to New York in the summer of 1963 ready to become a full-time political activist. During the next four
years, three of them in New York, I did, in fact, become
involved in dozens of political causes and groups, and in
activities which, at times, consumed my energies almost
full time.

When I began this book—four months after we arrived in Spéracèdes—I had expected that the bulk of it
would be about my political activities during these years.
Doctor Spock, Mitch Goodman, and the three others had
recently been indicted for conspiracy to violate the selective service law (for giving support to draft resisters)—
and this indictment derived indirectly from a campaign I
had started at Stanford University the previous spring. I

had come to Spéracèdes in order to write a novel, but once there a familiar pattern repeated itself; I found (felt) —again—that things political (my activities of the previous years) threatened to overrun and destroy my fiction. In order to deal with my political activities—to put them to rest—I wrote several long political articles during my first months in Spéracèdes. The articles weren't enough, though, and once again I found myself launched on a book-length project, one I thought would be political in nature, and one whose ultimate purpose, again, would be to exorcise (to explain) the political emotions I'd been carrying around in me so that—the material made tangible, dealt with in print—I could get on, could feel free to return to fiction, to a new novel.

The beginning point (GM) and the end point (the Spock trial) were there, and I only, I thought, had to describe a few of the events in my life which had led from one to the other—particularly my political involvements during the years 1963–67. By the time, in the fall of 1968, that I came to write about these years, though, I found that they didn't interest me, that all of the items I'd listed, made notes on, been ready to describe in detail, seemed unimportant.

My political activities—which I'd thought would be the most important part of the book—now seemed only parentheses between General Motors and Spéracèdes.

The narrative I was at work on, as the thoughts I put on paper the week of my thirtieth birthday showed me, was itself becoming less and less political. The more solidly I made my way into the world of politics during the years 1963–67, the more abstract, the more boring (in my memory) all the activities began to seem. Having made the decision to leave America just before major actions which I had helped plan, I had to wonder—especially as I became more and more at home in the daily life of

Spéracèdes, as I felt less and less desire to return to America, to become involved politically—how political I had ever been.

Politics was supposed to be that activity which dealt with the possible, with the "real" world—yet, in my memory, my own political activities didn't seem real. I felt a distaste for them, a revulsion to writing about them. And with this revulsion, with the necessity to write about my involvements, came one possibility: that all my political activities—even what I referred to as my political emotions—had been only one affect of my writing, of my desire to be a writer.

Such a feeling was mixed with (a rationalization for?) my sense of hopelessness about all political activity in America; read-ins, teach-ins, protest marches, draft card burnings, ads in *The New York Times* or the *Palo Alto Times*—what, I began to wonder, had these ever had to do with murder and suffering, war and revolution? If I found that the most overtly political part of my journey during the previous ten years was now the most boring, I also found (had to find) that it was the least significant. The more I was able (as in Indiana) to gain control over the rage that had first driven me to become involved politically—the more, that is, I was able to act "realistically" and regularly to achieve concrete objectives—the more, in my memory, all my activities seemed unreal, hopelessly cut off from the conditions which had first inspired them.

In the fall of 1963, however, such thoughts, literally, could not enter my mind. I was working on a new novel, I was working politically (with CORE, with antiwar groups), I was (this to pay for $150 monthly phone bills Betsey and I began to run up between Bloomington and New York) teaching blacks and Puerto Ricans in junior high schools in New York ghetto areas (Williamsburg, the

West Side, south Harlem). I was twenty-five years old, I'd had three articles published, I'd written seven unpublished books, and, in my one-room apartment on the fifth floor of a West Side brownstone, I led the life of a New York writer, of a New York intellectual involved in left-wing activities. On the days I didn't teach, I'd stay home and write, and keep in shape by going up and down the five flights to see if the mail had come, with its daily letter from Betsey, its daily batch of rejections. (There was a balcony under my window and I couldn't see to the sidewalk below the house; the mail came anywhere from nine to eleven-thirty.)

Above my desk I kept a scoreboard—a list of where each of my books, stories, and articles was, the date each had been sent out, and the odds. (These ranged, depending on my mood, from 10–1 or 15–1 for a story I felt confident about, to 989,989–1 for the film rights to an unsold novel.) At the bottom of the scoreboard I listed a Best Bet, Hopeful, Long Shot, Sleeper, and a Daily Double— and I kept a running count of rejections and acceptances —THEM vs. US. Once a day my friend Jerry Charyn would call, or I'd call him (we'd gone to Columbia together and he'd had his first story taken by *Commentary* the previous winter)—"How many pages today, Jay?" he'd ask. "Six," I'd say. "Better get back to work," he'd reply. "I did seven."

During the afternoons I'd play basketball in Central Park, and two or three evenings a week I'd be at a political meeting of one kind or another. If, for a while, my silent politics had been irresponsible, mad, and uncompromisingly radical, I found, back in New York, that I had swung to the other extreme: in things political, I now became realistic, responsible, sane. Thus, though I was signing statements that fall, before Kennedy's death, in which I declared I wouldn't serve in Vietnam, and in which I urged others not to—I was working, during the following spring and summer for the (re)election of those (the "lesser of two evils") who were sending men to Vietnam. Though I still believed in immediate equality for all men, in immediate withdrawal of U.S. forces from Vietnam, I was able to speak to groups about the need to write to their congressmen in order to urge de-escalation of the war, or passage of the voting rights bill.

During the spring and summer of 1964 I worked with Lower East Side CORE in voter registration. I still see the looks on the faces of the Puerto Ricans who answered doors—their fear, their shame, eyes lowered, as they said, as if they'd all agreed on a single response: "Spanish don't vote."

I remember how quickly I became immune to the rot and odors of their buildings. I remember their politeness (excessive—nobody living in such conditions, I said, should be polite), the times I was invited in for something to eat, to drink—and the thrill when we'd be able to convince a single man or woman to go with us to the local firehouse to register. Most of all, though, I remember that we worked that summer to get them to register so that they could vote for Lyndon Baines Johnson.

My job, as I saw it on my return to New York, on behalf of any cause, became an eminently American one: to win friends and influence people. This could best be accomplished by demonstrating something that was equally American: that what was morally right was also pragmatically profitable. (E.g., it was in America's "self-interest" to get out of Vietnam.)

I met obstacles—facts which, a year or two before would have returned me to the letter to Kennedy, and the memory of which, in Spéracèdes, helped account for my desire to reject what I'd been part of. I remember, for example, talking with friends in the spring of 1964 about the "stall-in" of automobiles that was being planned for opening day of the New York World's Fair by militant CORE chapters. My friends—like most liberals, like most civil rights leaders, like the *New York Post* and *Times*— opposed the stall-in. This was "going too far." There were, I was told endlessly, peaceful, orderly ways of registering grievances, working against injustice. Moreover, my friends argued, hadn't the passage of a civil rights bill, hadn't the March on Washington, the victories of Martin Luther King—hadn't these shown that things were changing, progressing? Most important, tying up New York's highways would only "alienate" those white people whose support Negroes had worked so hard to gain and whose support "they would need" to achieve further gains.

I asked some of my students at a junior high in south Harlem about the stall-in. Most of them didn't know anything about it—those who did seemed to agree with my friends. A few, however, dissented. One seventh-grade boy wrote: "If a man not going to be my friend cause he gets held up in a traffic jam for some hours one afternoon he must not be a very good friend in the first place."

I remember also, during my first year back in New York, working with a friend, Gene Glickman, on a mass income tax refusal campaign which (again) was to be national in scope. We drew up a plan, drafted a covering letter, met with a lawyer, and then sent out dozens of letters to friends we thought would be sympathetic to the idea. So as to draw in "moderates," we stated that the taxes would be placed in escrow until the United States government was involved in negotiations on Vietnam, or had been rebuffed in an honest attempt to get negotiations going. Also, that—so as to minimize personal risk—the tax refusal would not be undertaken or announced until five thousand people had pledged themselves to it.

Not a single response was positive. Though such experiences confirmed some deeply skeptical part of me, at the time they only made me work harder in a "realistic" way, they only made me work to do away with those things whose continuance threatened to make me radical in action as well as belief.

Betsey and I were married in the early summer of 1964 and we moved nine blocks south to a brownstone apartment on West Seventy-sixth Street. By then I had finished the novel I'd begun the previous fall and I'd also had—a few months before we were married—two short stories accepted (one by *The Colorado Quarterly*, the other by *Transatlantic Review*), the first fiction of mine that had been taken for publication since I'd begun submitting material seven years before. By this time I'd had, by count, over five hundred rejections—and nothing, not even the impersonality of the acceptances, could dampen my joy (one of the acceptances—for ten dollars—came on a mimeographed form; the other began: "I wonder if we ever told you we'd like to do your story? Would our usual $25 be acceptable?").

I'd attended no regular classes at Columbia that year, and taken none of the requisite exams along the Ph. D. route. In May, I applied for a part-time teaching job in Columbia College, one supposedly given only to graduate students who had already passed their "orals" and were at work on their dissertations. When the head of the department questioned me about my progress toward the Ph. D., I mumbled something about taking the "orals" the following year. "And if you start another novel—?" he asked. I shrugged, smiled, got the job, and shortly after classes started in September, began work on another novel. It was one I'd been planning, trying to start for over a year and a half.

I taught at Columbia for the next two years (my office during my second year was the one that Mark and

Charles Van Doren had shared, across from Richard
Chase's), and found at first that I enjoyed the teaching,
enjoyed the fact of being in the position (at twenty-six) of
those I'd admired most in the world when I'd been seventeen. The men who had, nine years before, seemed like
gods to me—Lionel Trilling, Andrew Chiappe, James
Shenton, F. W. Dupee—were now—the word had a won-
derfully snobbish sound to it—colleagues.

I found, though, that the life at Columbia, once I
could be part of it, held little interest for me—I did my
work and got paid for it, and spent as little time on campus as I had to. Though it was supposedly against Columbia's rules, I continued to do substitute teaching in the
city schools, and this teaching was more important to me.

Yet, in Spéracèdes, when I came to write about my
teaching of black and Puerto Rican students, I found that
I didn't want to—and again, now, back in America, I find
that I resist detailing any experiences, friendships, anecdotes. To do so would, I claim, be only additional exploitation of their lives. If I filled a book with stories, with
my students' compositions, and we read them, we would
all, I suppose—even me—be moved; we might even vow
to "do something"—but what could we do? The individual success I may have had during those years, the effect
I might have had on a few students (and their effect on
me)—what does this have to do with the problems of massive numbers of human beings trapped in massive school
systems within massive social and economic systems?

GM again. During my days in the city schools the
refrain—without revolution, America is doomed—was
stronger than it had ever been. Still, I resist trotting out
the lives of black and Puerto Rican students I knew, I resist catering to what I feel is nothing more than the moral
voyeurism of well-intentioned liberal readers, I resist
providing a bit more of what Huck Finn would have

called "soul butter." For what warnings could I preface
any extended account of these teaching experiences with
that would be powerful enough to counteract the illusion
that my account would produce—i.e., that if only there
were enough such books (enough such teachers, enough
such publicity), all might still be changed, improved.

Nothing I could say, no memories I could conjure up
would be more than a footnote to what I felt the first day
I entered a ghetto school: that it was sheer madness to
believe that what was needed to make things right would
ever come from the things, the institutions which had
made them wrong; that one could not—that I should not
—ever try to argue about this.

As always, one did the best one could—I continued
to act "realistically" to try to change particular wrongs, to
create options, alternatives—but there was more hope, I
felt, not only for the children trapped in the schools, but
even more for those of us who were not poor, black, and
young—in blowing up the schools (the ghettos) and starting over, than there was in continuing with things as they
were, with trying to institute reforms from within, via the
means available.

What, I wondered, were children doing in such
places? What was miraculous, what mystified, even excited me—was not that the students knew so little, but
that, given the world they'd made their way in, they
knew anything at all, that they were still alive, still individual, unique, different—one from the other.

But I stop here, before the anecdotes and editorials
rush from me. (The picture that has been in my head
while writing all of this seems to counter the seriousness
with which I want to tell all, with which I want to resist
telling all: an eighth-grade class lined up to leave the
room at the end of the period, and as I glance at them I
notice that one of the boys in the back of the double line

has his arm around his girlfriend, his hand resting on her breast, fondling it. He sees that I see him, start to move toward him, and he smiles at me, as if to say—everything's okay, man. He winks at me, knowingly; I stop, smile, wink back.) For even if I could arouse read-ers—could make them feel deeply about the children of the ghettos—what point? The liberal's notion (wish) that understanding and love and goodwill and education will eventually solve all problems becomes, in America, only another version of the conservative's notion that before we change anything else, as Barry Goldwater was telling me in 1960, "we must first change the hearts of men." The effect of both is to sustain the status quo.

The political and the personal, if they are ever sepa-rate for me, are certainly not separate here: i.e., I stop myself from further description and/or analysis out of the knowledge of how deeply these experiences and impres-sions went, out of the knowledge that these experiences —more directly than others—found transformation in my fiction (though here, as opposed to my letter to Kennedy, the fact came before the fiction); out of the feeling that the black children I've known have in some way been the brother I'd loved, felt guilty toward, wanted to help, to love, and—losing guilt—to be equal to (me to him, him to me).

I taught, I wrote, I played ball, Betsey and I enjoyed living on the West Side (she got a job as a children's li-brarian at the Brooklyn Public Library, where I'd first discovered books), I became increasingly active in poli-tics, and in New York's chief political activity, political discussion. If the way to return to the real world lay in compromising my revolutionary vision, then the way to continue to make my way in this world also lay in compromise. I became a "respectable" activist—trying to persuade those to the right of me to move slightly left and those to the left of me to move slightly right. I was reasonable, realistic—I never appeared in a public demonstration without a jacket, tie, fresh haircut. The way to accomplish all objectives, I was learning, was to gain the goodwill of moderate Americans; and anything which threatened to alienate them became the gravest of political sins. In the antiwar movement, for example, one acted on the assumption that if only we could educate something called "The American People" about the war in Vietnam, they would come to oppose it; if they came to oppose it, they would make their voices heard; and if they made their voices heard, the government would execute their will and end the war. What I'd learned my second time in Indiana took precedence over what I'd felt my first time there.

I remember, for example, in the fall of 1965, attending the first meeting of the Committee of the Professions to End the War in Vietnam, and earning myself a nomination to the steering committee of one of the subcommittees (The Committee to Organize an International Conference of Intellectuals on the War in Vietnam) by arguing against the participation of Communists (e.g., Yevtushenko) in the International Conference.

We had, I insisted, to keep our principal objective in mind: how would the mass media treat the conference? If there were Communists invited wouldn't this give the media the opportunity they were looking for to malign us and to ignore the force of our arguments against the war? The reason we professionals (artists, writers, lawyers, doctors, teachers, et al.) had come to that meeting was, I declared, to form a "new" kind of antiwar organization that would be "effective" precisely because it would be immune from the attacks usually leveled against left-wing organizations. Our job, in short, was to make antiwar activity "respectable."

Although I wanted to feel that my political views were closer to those of more radical organizations, I was at home in the Committee of the Professions. Yes, I agreed with those to my left, it was regrettable that we had to try to make antiwar activity "respectable"; yes, we should probably direct our attention to changing those things which made such compromises, tactics necessary —but first we had to do everything possible to try to end the war in Vietnam, and this meant trying to build a "mass popular movement," this meant trying to make our cause seem legitimate in the eyes of "The American People."

I remember sitting around tables in comfortable East and West Side apartments (from my position as co-chairman of the International Conference Committee I had been made a permanent member of the steering committee of the Committee of the Professions), drawing up lists of the most prominent intellectuals in the world, discussing their relative merits, deciding which of them we should invite to the International Conference, figuring out which of us were friends with them, which of us had friends who were friends with them. I drafted the letter that went to them, and we all complimented ourselves when replies (from Mumford, Sartre, Niemöller, Russell, Toynbee, et al.) began coming in.

I also remember getting the Committee to back one of my proposals: for a national advertising and fund-raising campaign on television. If we wanted to reach the American people, I said, then why not do it in an American way, with one-minute spots coast-to-coast by prominent individuals, in prime time. I was guaranteed funds by the Committee, prominent individuals, a sympathetic ad agency to handle things—and I began contacting the major TV networks—only to discover that they would accept no political advertising whatever, except as part of the campaign of a legitimate political candidate during an election year. To work through the courts to force the networks to take antiwar ads, or to try to get the FCC to rule that they had to—everyone we consulted was of the same opinion: forget it.

From time to time I wrote articles about the war, about the antiwar movement, about the civil rights movement—and in the Committee of the Professions I was (more so than at Columbia) thought of as a writer; people discussed my ideas with me, inquired about my fiction and my articles, read my stories. I remember helping to organize the first of the nation's read-ins, sponsored by the Committee of the Professions—composing letters, ads, making arrangements with Town Hall—and thinking all the time of the day when someone like myself would be doing the secretarial work and I (with Mailer, Malamud, Miller, Kazin, Lowell) would be asked to read from my works. (This was now something less than a grandiose fantasy, I told myself, since the novel—*Big Man*—I'd completed during my first year of marriage—I'd worked on it for two and a half years—had been accepted for publication.)

I enjoyed—in somewhat the same way I'd done so the last time I'd been in New York—being an anonymous helper in "the movement." The first job I did for the Committee of the Professions was to pick up and deliver its stationery. And I also enjoyed New York name-dropping games, being "in" on things literary. When, for example, during the Town Hall read-in, one of the speakers chose not to read from her own works, but instead to explain to the audience, as spokesman for *all* the other writers, poets, and actors, why the read-in was taking place, why she and the others had chosen to protest the war in this particular manner, I could smile, gossip to friends; she had telephoned our office a week before the read-in to ask why she had not been invited. When she'd been told that we already had too many participants, she'd insisted until we'd reluctantly agreed to let her have five minutes of stage time. She took twenty.

I seem always to have been soliciting signatures and money for ads in *The New York Times*. Generally, faculty members who refused to sign refused because, although they were, they assured me, "against the war," they did not agree "completely" with the text of our ad. If they could suggest some revisions . . . if the wording could be changed to represent more accurately their viewpoint . . . One well-known professor in Columbia's English Department looked first at a list of signers and, without reading the text, returned the sheet to me; he would not, he said, sign an ad that had already been signed by Allen Ginsberg.

One particular ad contained over six thousand signatures, took up three pages of *The News of the Week in Review*, and was the largest political ad that had ever, until that time, been bought for the *Times*. We received wire-service stories, we were able—from contributions that came in because of the ad—to reprint it in a dozen other cities, to spend an evening debating the choice of these cities. For a time I suppose I felt that six thousand signatures in the Sunday *Times*, or several dozen prominent intellectuals reading from their work at Town Hall somehow related to what was happening in Washington or Saigon.

My writing went well in New York. The more I acted in the world of "real" politics, the more I was willing to compromise my political vision in order to obtain specific objectives, the less, it seemed, I felt a need to compromise the vision that informed my novels and stories. Though I was, I told myself, no less enraged by the world than I'd been before, I was now able to deal with this rage (in both my fiction and my politics) in an efficient, objective way. The process reinforced itself endlessly: the more control I gained over my rage, the more I came to believe in this control and in the power it gave me. The more regularly I put myself into ongoing political activities, the more I came to believe that my ability to have a specific effect on other individuals (and/or a few events) mattered; and the more this happened (as it did in the Committee of the Professions), the more I taught myself that with this power came—the favorite word of the newspapers I'd been brought up with— "responsibility."

As always in such things I had involved inner theories to justify and explain (to myself) everything I did— this time, however, I found that I had little need to use my own sources of rationalization. What I did and said was approved—and protected—by the world I moved in, by those who agreed with me and worked with me, and by those who did not—but who would have defended to the death, as I saw it, my right to have compromised my more absolute demands and revolutionary desires.

What I remember most when I think of my three years in New York are meetings, and what I remember most about the meetings is that there were so many of them. Not long after I'd begun working with the Committee of the Professions I was selected to be their representative to the nation's largest antiwar group—the Fifth Avenue Vietnam Peace Parade Committee, and early in 1966 I was made a member of the executive committee of this committee.

Although Parade Committee meetings now seem indistinguishable, one from the other, I do recall the first meeting I attended. It was held in a run-down building near Union Square, and the meeting room was long, narrow, smoke-filled. We sat on wooden chairs, and as the arguments and speeches spun around me (the Committee was composed of representatives from over eighty New York antiwar groups) I felt as if I'd been sent back in a time machine, dropped into a romantic era when words like Working Class and Trotskyite and The Masses still had meaning.

I was surprised that there were so many different groups organized against the war—even more surprised by the fury with which they attacked one another. Delegates spent most of their time denouncing one another—as if, it seemed, rival antiwar groups were more insidious enemies than Dean Rusk or Lyndon Johnson. At the same time, I was astonished by the tolerance and endurance of the representatives: I never—even after months of meetings—could understand how so many people could sit so long, so patiently through endless hours of what seemed to be the same old debates.

At my first meeting there seemed to me to be an infinite number of motions, votes, appeals to Roberts Rules of Order ("Point of Information" was the standard procedure for interrupting in order to make a speech on any subject whatever). One little old woman lectured us for ten minutes on the evils of war; another told us why the war in Vietnam should be ended; a third told us about a tea party she'd held in her apartment in the Bronx, to which she'd invited her neighbors—the response of these neighbors to a discussion on Vietnam "proved," she said, that "the American people were rising up against the war."

The person who sat next to me—an intense gray-haired representative wearing thick glasses, who, despite his hair, seemed to be in his late twenties, spoke to no one, didn't respond to the few attempts at conversation I offered, and sat through three or four hours of the meeting staring fiercely ahead until, at one point, he suddenly rose from his chair and with a sweep of his arm which almost knocked me from mine, his fists beating the air, he proclaimed through the smoke—"What we must all do, comrades, is to educate the working men of America to the fact that their true enemy lives in Washington! We must rip the mask off the bloody tyrant and let the American people see his murderous face! . . ."

Five minutes later he sat down—and while representatives actually argued for or against what he had said (it was in the form of a proposition, or an amendment to a proposition—I can't recall which), he returned to his former expressionless pose, staring silently ahead.

What surprised me most afterwards was the fact that some decisions had actually been made at the meeting. Those we thought we were struggling against, I recall thinking, were surely not handicapped by such fierce and insane allegiance to democratic procedures.

Although at the time I kept vowing to quit—kept telling myself how mad the meetings were, how nothing was being gained by all the fights, or even by the marches, I stayed on; and when I think of the Parade Committee now I find that I do so with some affection: I think of the pleasant sensation at seeing my name—on letterheads, handbills, and ads—alphabetically trapped between those of Otto Nathan and Grace Paley. I recall also, at the close of one meeting, being approached by a short, balding man in his sixties or seventies. He shook my hand warmly and thanked me for having supported his group's position during the meeting. "It seems to me, though, young man," he went on, "that you have some significant gaps in your education." He smiled and put his hand on my arm. "I was wondering if you have ever heard of the six hundred families?" I said no. His smile was broader. "Perhaps," he suggested, "we can get together some evening and I can explain to you just how America's ruling class works. . . ."

By the spring of 1966, my confidence built up by my activities on the executive committees of two of the nation's major antiwar groups—I began advocating direct action against the war. With the growth of both the war and the antiwar movement, some form of mass civil disobedience, I felt, was necessary and possible.

When I brought the subject up at Committee of the Professions meetings, however, nobody was enthusiastic. Less than that: they seemed offended by the suggestion —as if sitting down on Fifth Avenue or at an induction center was something below them, something vulgar. When, somewhat earlier that year, I'd tried to get the Committee of the Professions to join forces with some civil rights groups—this was before people such as Martin Luther King, and organizations such as CORE had joined the antiwar protests—the results had been disastrous. I invited representatives of a Harlem group to a meeting and the discussions took a wrong turn when the Harlem people made some remarks about how they had been double-dealt in the past by white liberals. "What," members of the committee kept asking me afterwards, "do those people *want?*"

At the Parade Committee there were groups and individuals who had always been ready to move from protest to action, but in the spring of 1966 even people such as Dave Dellinger, chairman of the Committee (and later chairman of the National Mobilization Committee, one of the first to actually get into the Pentagon in the fall of 1967) were insisting that the time was "not yet ripe" for mass tactics involving civil disobedience: SANE would drop out, the Committee would be split, we would lose the bulk of our middle-class constituency, we would alienate moderates, the uncommitted.

After this, though I still tried to persuade "moderates" (in the manner of Draper, Fulbright, Schlesinger, Lippmann) of the immorality and impracticality of the war, I did so with less enthusiasm. The more I knew about Vietnam, and the more I argued about it—the less I wanted to argue, to know. My political activities began to seem meaningless, distasteful. If those who were most actively opposed to the war were still unwilling to go further than legitimate protest, what hope was there? The reasoning which had sustained my own antiwar involvement until then—that even if we'd had no effect on stopping the war, we (the peace movement) had put brakes on its escalation, we'd provided Lyndon Johnson with breathing space—with more options should he have decided he wanted to get out of Vietnam—the consolation that derived from such thoughts was unsatisfying, unconnected with what was going on in Vietnam. Once again, a plan of mine thwarted, I began to withdraw into myself. Everything I saw or felt (in the newspapers, in the ghetto schools, in the apartments of New York liberals) helped return me to the state of mind that had prevailed during my months in Indianapolis—this time, however, my depression led to no new political campaign. Things seemed, quite simply, hopeless; just as three hundred years of racism and exploitation weren't going to be changed by civil rights bills and poverty programs, empire was not going to be stopped by advertisements, or genocide by court battles.

Though I continued in the spring and summer of 1966 to work at any task and with any group that was trying to end this particular war, I began to believe that there were some things about which nothing could be done, and that Vietnam was one of them. The activities of the previous year (I was, by then, attending meetings five and six nights a week) bored me now, tired me—I wanted to get away from it all, to be far from meetings and marches. As long as I stayed in America, though, I knew I would continue to work against the war—but the only effect of my work, I felt, would be to drain me. (Although I'd written several stories and articles, since *Big Man* had been accepted—almost a year before—I'd been unable to begin a new novel.)

The majority of Americans were comfortable, secure, untouched by the war in any direct way. They would, therefore, continue to acquiesce to anything the government did in their name. Those who opposed the war were not, in significant numbers, prepared to undertake the risks involved in escalating their protests. The government, I concluded, knew then that it could continue to do whatever it wanted. More than this, I began to feel that protest against the war was actually welcomed by the government—proof of those American freedoms for which American boys were dying.

Betsey and I talked of leaving the country: I would begin work on another novel, I would be away from New York, I would be far from those political involvements which, though I couldn't separate myself from them, I felt could destroy my fiction—and, therefore, me.

If, by my actual and sustained involvement in politics I had lost my more extreme desires, I had also lost, by this same involvement, the hopes—the dream—that had first led me to political activity. I was left, I felt, without illusion about my ability to change the world— and without anything to do. I didn't need, for the conditions of my own life, a revolution; I was no longer able, it seemed, to compensate for my helplessness and despair with dreams and schemes of omnipotence. My losses seemed, at the time, heavy, sad, final.

That my political involvements had come to bore me was not so surprising, though; how, after all, could any

political activity in the real world compare with the political campaign I'd created in the months following GM?
While events in the real world—in Vietnam or at home or
at a south Harlem junior high—could now propel me to
"appropriate" action in the real world, they still did so, at
least partially, so that my fiction would remain free of
these events, would go beyond them—i.e., I still acted politically in order to exorcise things I thought of as being
merely political—so that, I told myself, my fiction would
not become didactic and journalistic. Since, in the five
years since my letter to Kennedy, my politics had become
less fictional, other things followed inevitably.

In the summer of 1966 I did no such theorizing. I
told Columbia that I wouldn't be teaching there in the
fall and Betsey and I made plans for spending a year in
Europe.

In the middle of the summer, Jerry Charyn called
from California to ask if I wanted to come to Stanford in
the fall as a writer-teacher. I said no, but the offer was
tempting (I would be a teacher *because* I was a writer).
When Albert Guérard called a week later and pointed
out that Europe would still be in the same place nine
months hence (and that I would have more money to
enjoy it), we changed our minds and decided he was
right: we would see California (something we'd talked of
before), we would put away more money, we would have
more time to plan our year (or two) in Europe—and, with
a light teaching schedule and without New York committees, I was certain that I could get to work again.

Big Man was published that August. When my editor called me on a broiling New York afternoon to say
that copies had arrived, I ran to the subway, and arrived
at the publisher's downtown office, dripping sweat, a
half hour later. It had been nine years since I'd begun
submitting novels; when my editor handed me a copy of

my first published book the only thing I could say was, "Gee—it's so thin."

A few weeks later, when the first reviews had appeared, I asked a salesman in E. J. Korvette's book department if he had a novel about basketball which I'd seen reviewed in the previous Sunday's *Times.* "Big something—I can't remember what—was the title," I told him. "You mean *Big Man,*" he said, and led me to where the book was. I tried to act nonchalant, interested. We talked. I asked if the book was good, if it was selling, and when his replies were affirmative, I turned the book to the back cover—tried to smile modestly, to apologize for having misled him—and showed him the picture of the author. "That's me," I said. "Oh," he replied. "Your uncle was in this morning—"

Less than a month after publication, in September, 1966, we left New York for California. At Stanford, I was soon at work on a novel (its settings: Williamsburg schools and the West Side of Manhattan)—I was also more relieved than I'd believed possible, simply to be away from the rush of New York meetings, protests, politics. Betsey and I rented a house in Palo Alto—with lemon and orange trees, wisteria, roses, magnolias, morning glories, lots of closets, and a room for me to work in —the first time I'd ever had a separate writing room; the pleasantness of the climate, the people, and the campus life made it easy for me, I found, to believe that there was no urgent need to do anything or try to change anything. My disillusionment with politics, moreover, seemed to reinforce what my political activities during the previous three years had helped stabilize: the trust I put in my fiction. Because nothing I did or wrote could have any significant effect on whatever real world lay beyond my fiction, I might as well, I told myself, do what I wanted and write novels. The guilt which had previously bound my politics to my writing seemed gone.

I let myself become involved in whatever campus antiwar protests presented themselves—but these were minimal. I attended meetings of the faculty peace committee held over lunch, outdoors, on the patio of the Student Union, and I was content, generally, to let others do most of the talking, organizing.

The Vietnam war, to judge from these meetings, seemed cause, not for action or outrage, but for academic debate. I remember attending four or five luncheons in a row, where a half-dozen faculty members worked at making a decision about bringing a speaker to the campus to "discuss" the war. The speaker's chief merit was to be his potential appeal to moderate faculty members. One faculty member vetoed Hans Morgenthau as being too controversial.

I let some people know that I found such activities absurdly inadequate, and some let me know that they agreed with me, that the campus had been more active in previous years (e.g., in a campaign against a nearby Redwood City napalm plant). But discussion that fall continued to be equal to action. The one suggestion I ventured —that the faculty urge draft resistance, that we "aid and abet" our students' refusal to serve in the military—was transformed, after much discussion, into an announcement I sent out that fifteen faculty members were available for "draft *counseling*." Our job, according to most of the faculty I was able to recruit for the counseling, was not to advocate any course of action, or to risk jail—but to try to "educate" our students about the war (a war we'd already been involved in for at least twelve years), to let them know, as one well-known professor put it, that in a nation which allowed dissent there was nothing "un-American" about "considering" Conscientious Objection.

Things went on like this for about half the year, and I didn't mind. Life was pleasant, untroubled. I taught, I wrote, I signed whatever petitions came to me, I was looked to as a writer. Most afternoons, after writing or teaching, Jerry Charyn and I would retrieve a bit of New York City schoolyard by playing paddle tennis with paddles Jerry had expropriated when he'd been a New York City Department of Parks "parkie." Vietnam was far away—distant, abstract, always something of an idea. Newspapers, film clips, photos—these could shorten the distance now and then, but the immediacy of the war, if it came at all, came intermittently and always seemed to need some self-starting provocation; one had to work hard to ignite a sense of horror, to remember that abstractions such as murder, suffering, and death had individual instances, and that it was for these individual instances that one had first protested.

The announcement, in January, that Vice President Hubert Humphrey was coming to the campus to speak, changed things, made Vietnam seem suddenly less distant. The campus was quickly in motion. An open meeting was called and the students who attended voted to walk out on Humphrey. The faculty who were present at the meeting pleaded (there, and after) for a more moderate action. A walkout, they said, would violate the Vice President's right to free speech; it would "alienate" that large body of uncommitted students and faculty we were seeking to educate; it would—the phrase I remember most—be "in bad taste."

A faculty group called its own meeting and decided on its own form of protest: those who were against the war would come to the auditorium to hear Humphrey, but they would remain silent throughout his speech, they would neither heckle nor applaud, and they would identify themselves as opponents of the war by wearing white armbands.

The faculty group issued a statement, which they ran as an ad in the student paper on the day of Humphrey's visit: "We, the undersigned members of the faculty, welcome Vice President Humphrey to Stanford, but in so doing we cannot allow our welcome to imply approval of the Administrations's resumption of the bombing of North Vietnam, extending a policy which Mr. Humphrey has unequivocally endorsed. . . ."

The decorous language of the faculty welcome pushed me over the edge, into action, anger. I began speaking around the campus—at meetings, rallies, at a marathon teach-in—and in my speeches I mocked the faculty armband statement, I said that Humphrey was a murderer, an agent of a murderous policy, and that to call him anything less was euphemism. The week of Humphrey's visit, I telephoned Charles Stein, a professor of statistics, and one of the faculty members I knew would find the armband welcome as repulsive as I had. We met with one of the student leaders, Barry Greenberg (head of the campus "free university"), and I brought a statement I'd drafted which urged a walkout and which condemned Humphrey and the administration he spoke for as "murderous and criminal." Within a few hours we had over two-dozen faculty signatures, and we ran our statement as an ad on the day Humphrey arrived. (The white armband ad was signed by 211 faculty.)

Earlier that year, in one of my freshman English classes, we had discussed selections from several autobiographical essays on childhood—by Baldwin, Yeats, Kazin, Stegner, Nabokov, and Howe. My students had remained typically unresponsive. They seemed to understand the

essays well enough, but they didn't react to them. When
I pressed them—this was after a discussion of *Notes of a
Native Son*—one girl finally blurted out, with the first gesture of emotion I'd seen to that point: "Childhood wasn't
like that!" The rest of the class nodded in agreement.
Weren't these writers, the girl asked, "exaggerating?" The
others echoed her question.

It wasn't that the students didn't believe what Baldwin and the others had told them (they did), or that they
had nothing in their own lives which could correspond to
what Baldwin had told them (they did not)—but something which seemed sadder: that they had nothing within
their experience which enabled them to *imagine* what had
been described for them. Stanford students were, generally, intelligent, liberal, good-natured, open, wholesome,
rich, and dull—archetypes of the WASP whom Erik Erikson has described as being "emotionally retentive."

The fact that Humphrey was going to be on this particular campus (a real agent of a real war, was the way I
put it in speeches) rekindled in me all the resentment I'd
felt earlier at the easy, insulated lives of the students, at
the absurdly academic forms of liberal protest—and, most
of all, at my own failure to have done much for half a
year. The fact, that, before Humphrey's visit, I would
have agreed with most people that if a government official was safe at any major university in America, it would
have been at Stanford—a week before his visit, Dow
Chemical, maker of napalm, was on the campus and
there had been no trouble—only gave me more reason to
try to start something.

On February 20, 1967, two years after we had first
begun the bombing of North Vietnam, Humphrey chose
as the subject for his opening remarks to the faculty and
students of the university often called "the Harvard of the
West," *Time* Magazine's "now generation" of that year.

He said he came to Stanford "to be where the action is," and, in his most memorable remark of the day, he referred to the late Pope John as one of the "now people." He did not mention Vietnam in his opening statement, and about seventy-five people walked out when he was done. A while later, when in answer to a question, he stated that "if President John F. Kennedy were alive today he would be doing exactly what the Johnson Administration is doing at this very hour," several hundred more people walked out.

Humphrey's remarks (broadcast to those outside on a PA system) and the frustration of many at not having had the chance to walk in in order to walk out (my own predicament)—on good evidence, many of us believed the audience had been "packed"—began to affect those of us outside the hall. We stationed groups at the various exits, and waited for the Vice President's departure. Bloomington again, only this time I was, I knew, not in a minority.

When the meeting was over and Humphrey used a Secret Service decoy where the largest crowd had gathered at the rear of the auditorium, in order to sneak out a side exit, several hundred of us ran after him, yelling "Shame! Shame! Shame!" continually. He was in the car before we got to him, and he drove away. That night the event seemed important enough (an "attack on the Vice President") to be carried on nationwide television.

The president of Stanford, J. W. Sterling, immediately issued a public apology to Humphrey in the name of the university, and tried to place the blame for the "attack" on "nonstudents." We responded one sunny afternoon a few days later by marching on his office bearing signs such as "Give Credit Where Credit is Due," and "We Are Not Nonstudents."

As before, I was at work at once on an article concerning the events I'd been involved in, and, again, the article was accepted by *The New Republic*. In their version it ended with my comment concerning the dramatic rise in antiwar activities on the Stanford campus:

> All of this should seem heartening—as it did at first. But then one must remind oneself that although, in individual enclaves, the peace movement may grow, in Vietnam the war grows faster. Within a week of Humphrey's visit, for the first time, we mined North Vietnamese rivers, we shelled North Vietnam from the Bay of Tonkin and from directly below the demilitarized zone, and we used paratroopers as 50,000 US troops invaded the alleged NLF stronghold in Zone C. As Humphrey had put it at Stanford, Hanoi will know "by the summer" [of 1967] that "the ball game is over."

The New Republic had, however—and I was furious about it—cut the final four paragraphs of my article; the part the entire article had been building to, the part I'd considered most important. In them I'd reiterated what I'd been saying in speeches on campus before and after Humphrey's visit—that, for those who meant to be serious about their opposition to the war, the time was long overdue to move from protest to resistance, from dissent to direct action. E.g., ten thousand professors signing ten thousand more ads meant nothing; ten thousand professors refusing to teach, ready to act—that might mean something else.

I had begun my article with a quote from an essay that was much talked about at the time, Noam Chomsky's "The Responsibility of Intellectuals." The "responsibility of intellectuals," Chomsky had said, was "to speak the truth and to expose lies." But it was also, as he inferred, and as I would write in an article for *Commonweal* that spring ("Disobedience Now!"), "to act on this truth, to do those things which neither convince the convinced, nor educate a few more citizens, but relate—on a large scale

—directly to that horror which goes on every day in Vietnam." The kind of mass direct action I had proposed in New York the previous year seemed, once again, necessary and possible.

On the campus, some of us began publicly urging those of draft age not to serve in the military, and we made it clear when we did so that this was a violation of the law. My own approach and rhetoric began to change. Whereas in previous years I had advocated draft refusal on moral and altruistic grounds, I now began making statements which, when I read them back in newspapers, or in press releases from the Stanford News Office, continually astonished me. The *San Francisco Chronicle* dubbed me the "professor-provocateur." I said things in public—outrageous, uncompromising (e.g., comparisons of U. S. and Nazi actions)—to hundreds of people, that I never would have dared say to a single person. In brief, if like many liberals I had begun by believing in civil disobedience because I loved my country, because I wanted, as those in the civil rights movement had, to demonstrate the depth of my desire to save what was good in it—I now began advocating direct action in order, I said, "to save the world *from* my country." Anything, I stated, which gave support to the United States was, in effect, "to give aid and comfort to the enemy."

At the time of the national mobilization against the war that April, I worked on campus with a "We Accuse" campaign the student radicals had organized concerning Stanford's complicity in military-industrial projects. The links of the university with the war (primarily through the Stanford Research Institute), with chemical and biological warfare research, and with the strategic hamlet program, were carefully documented.

The faculty reaction to the "We Accuse" campaign was, again, disapproving. The posters—pictures of Presi-

dent Sterling and members of the Board of Trustees such
as David Packard, with WE ACCUSE written across the bottom, and collages of wounded Vietnamese children, of
burned villages, of dead soldiers behind them—were denounced by most students and faculty, and by the student
paper, again, as being "in bad taste." At a major rally that
week, from the entire faculty, the students could get only
Mitchell Goodman and me to speak publicly on behalf of
the campaign.

I tried to put things in perspective, to put brakes on
my activity, my rage: if we couldn't get more than a
handful of faculty and students at a major university to
endorse a few *posters*, what danger, really, did we—or
the entire antiwar movement—pose to the work that was
actually going on in military-research projects? I was not,
in fact, very interested in denouncing President Sterling.
He was probably, I pointed out in speeches and discussions, an "honorable man"—as were the stockholders in
military-production corporations, the members of the
Board of Trustees, the faculty who did the research. Most
of these people probably regretted the fact that we were
killing people in Vietnam; they probably believed they
wanted an end to the war. They were probably all "honorable men." But Chomsky was right—at the least, we
had to speak the truth, and the truth, as I saw it, was that
the president of Stanford and his assistants and the members of the Board of Trustees and those who did the research were the men in our immediate community who
made the decisions and handled the money and signed
the contracts which provided for the research and sustained the factories which made the weapons that went
to Vietnam and killed people.

The week-long series of tribunals, exposés, and rallies
was not "successful" in terms of winning friends—we
could get only fifty students and three faculty to march

on the Stanford Research Institute with us the afternoon
of the major rally—but they did, I was convinced, influence people. Though our campaigns seemed to make us
lose the support of "moderates," I was convinced that this
loss was temporary. I felt optimistic, certain that just as
those who had originally been against the walkout had
come to approve it, so those who denounced the "We Accuse" campaign would eventually understand it and endorse it. At the least, we started people on their first steps
toward recognizing—or even considering—the complicity
of the university, by its daily business, in war crimes, and
to considering this in a way that might not otherwise
have occurred to them. Our irresponsibility seemed quite
responsible to me.°

Buoyed—or deluded—by the intensity of my own activity, and by the amount of activity around me, I felt, at
the time, that it was almost impossible to be too radical.
The further left one moved, the more those in the middle
seemed to be drawn leftward.

In New York that week we had gone beyond the
dreams any of us had had a year or two before—
somewhere between three hundred thousand and a half
million people protested (I could remember marches in
which we'd been pleased that our numbers had doubled
—from five to ten thousand); in San Francisco we more
than filled the seventy thousand seats in Kezar Stadium.
The fact of such numbers, I felt, made certain things possible, and the argument I began advancing, became a sta-

---

° In the epilogue to *The Autobiography of Malcolm X*, Alex Haley
tells the following anecdote: "At the church where he would speak,
Malcolm X was seated on the platform next to Mrs. Martin Luther
King, to whom he leaned and whispered that he was 'trying to help,'
she told *Jet*. 'He said he wanted to present an alternative; that it might
be easier for whites to accept Martin's proposals after hearing him [Mal-
colm X]. I didn't understand him at first,' said Mrs. King. 'He seemed
rather anxious to let Martin know he was not causing trouble or making
it difficult, but that he was trying to make it easier. . . .'"

tistical, a pragmatic one: if, I claimed, only 10 percent of those who were in the East and West Coast marches were now ready for direct action, then at least two things were true: 1) there were between thirty and fifty thousand people who would with their bodies, be ready to stop the progress of the war at specific points (the Pentagon, Port Chicago, major induction centers), and 2) there would be enough antiwar personnel left (i.e., the remaining 90 percent) so that all ongoing "traditional" protests could continue at more than full strength.

This meant, moreover, that I no longer had to try to convince the unconvinced about anything concerning the war—my job, instead, was to search out those (the hypothetical 10 percent) who already agreed with me. The difference was crucial, I claimed, for it allowed many of us to abandon certain forms of liberal rhetoric and practice —we no longer had to worry about "alienating" moderates.

From this point on, throughout the spring and summer, I spent all my free time trying to organize a national campaign for mass civil disobedience—and I was able, during those months, to believe that I had a chance of succeeding, that we had a chance of doing something which could actually bring about an end to the war.

Something else: what had been true for my fiction now became true for my politics—I had only to do and say and write what I wanted. I no longer felt that I had to compromise my political vision in order that my fiction remain, in some way, free. I no longer had to try to convince others of what seemed obvious, beyond argument. Those I had to organize, those I would try to convince concerning tactics, already shared basic assumptions with me—about the horror of the war, about the need to do something commensurate with this horror.

I no longer had to do what I'd sometimes felt I had

to do—what I've feared, even while writing this book, I might feel compelled to do again; i.e., I no longer felt any need to justify my actions, to try to demonstrate why I was opposed to the war and how deeply I was opposed to it. I no longer felt any need to argue against the cynical accusation (one was against the war because it was fashionable to be against the war, because—as a committed [and committeed] member of the Left such a position was mandatory) which had usually been in the air, and against which I was always expected to argue. In previous years, especially among those who would claim, as if this made them the most liberal and open-minded of Americans, that "they had not yet made up their minds" about the war (if there were "two sides" to a story, it seemed to follow logically that neither could ever be right), I'd sometimes felt that I'd been expected to do more than argue, that I'd been expected to perform: to show—with eyes and voice and gesture—just how deeply, how sincerely my commitment to peace was.

In the spring of 1967 things were suddenly different. Immediately following the April 15th march I called a meeting of several members of the faculty antiwar committee at Stanford and found a sympathetic response to the idea of mass civil disobedience. A half-dozen faculty members signed an initial call I'd drawn up, which I then revised, and sent out, along with two covering letters.

Within a day we had sixteen endorsements, including several from faculty who had, only two months before, condemned the walkout on Humphrey. I remember, for example, going in to see one of the organizers of the white armband protest, and showing him the civil disobedience pledge. He read it and nodded. "Of course I'll sign," he said. "But I was wondering," he added at once, "—have you ever considered sabotage?"

The tone of the pledge to civil disobedience was indicative of my hopefulness: "We do not want to protest the war any longer," it said at one point, "we want to stop it. We are prepared, through mass civil disobedience to say NO to our government. . . ." Using the English Department mimeograph machine, I ran off the pledge, a list of its sixteen signers, and a covering letter. I sent these to the entire faculty and staff—and additional endorsements began coming in at once.

Encouraged by this response, I called a meeting of antiwar faculty groups from other bay area colleges (Berkeley, San Francisco State, San José State). The professors from these colleges, though surprised at the number of civil disobedience pledges we'd already received at Stanford, were unenthusiastic. Several hours, as I recall the evening, were spent in tearing apart our pledge, sentence by sentence. The vagueness of our objectives aroused fierce denunciations, wild arguments—civil disobedience against what? How could a Stanford faculty group organize a nationwide campaign? Shutting down the Pentagon, major induction centers—? This was dangerous talk, wishful thinking. To my repeated explanation —the targets could only be specified exactly when we knew our numbers—the obvious response was flung back: until we know the targets, how can we pledge to act?

One "uncommitted" member of the Stanford faculty interrupted the arguments regularly every half hour by suddenly jumping up and declaring: "All right, I'll sign—!" He would then give all the reasons for his decision to sign, only to interrupt at the next half hour to tell us that he had changed his mind, that he could not sign such a document, and why. Several times Mitch Goodman interrupted by shouting (to middle-aged professors he didn't know)—"I'm disgusted with all of you!"

Our initial objective had been to get about twenty faculty to pledge themselves to break the law—i.e., to enlist about 10 percent of those who had previously shown some form of opposition to the war; if the 10 percent ratio held at an enclave as conservative as Stanford, we would, I claimed, have no trouble in getting the movement going nationwide.

Within a month of the April 15 march, we had about fifty pledges, many from the most prominent faculty at the university. We held a press conference and we received excellent coverage—good spots on radio and television, and page one stories in newspapers throughout the West (e.g., a *San José Mercury* headline: AT STANFORD: GOVERNMENT OBSTRUCTION PLOT HATCHED). On the campus students told me that the news had "blown people's minds." Fifty Stanford faculty members committing civil disobedience and going to jail—? If this were true, anything was possible.

I was more confident than I'd ever been before, though I do remember, when a TV reporter asked me at the press conference why we thought we would "succeed" where others had failed, replying with what seemed to me, then, to be the truth: that we didn't, of course, know whether or not we would "succeed"—we hoped we would succeed, but what we were doing was more an "act of faith" than anything else—we would act *as if* we thought that what we did could end the war. What else could we do?

By this time we had also, I thought, replied to one of the major objections the faculty from the other colleges had put to us—how were we going to get the campaign going nationwide? When we had shown the results of our month's work to Chester Hartman, the acting director of Vietnam Summer, he'd been enthusiastic and had encouraged us. Vietnam Summer, a coalition which was to be the antiwar equivalent of Mississippi Summer, had just been organized, and it had the money and prestige (Mar-

tin Luther King was behind it, the Kennedys and Rocke-
fellers were supposedly giving it secret support) to put
the kind of national campaign we talked about into action. We could state at our press conference, then, as the
news media reported, that we had "conferred with the
head of a major antiwar group with facilities and contacts
sufficient to support the movement," and we could quote
from a memo Hartman had sent us:

> . . . The "We Won't Go" movement among draft-age
> youth represents an extreme, potentially effective, and
> apparently infectious development in the society. . . .
> There is a great need for an analogous activity on the
> part of those who are past draft age. . . . The response
> that people at Stanford have had among that faculty to
> the notion of civil disobedience against the war suggests
> that it is an idea whose time has come . . .

Hartman's memo also outlined a plan of action: We
would send out mass mailings stating the case for civil
disobedience in June, we would analyze the responses,
we would then select the most appropriate actions and
targets, recruit the key leaders, and, in late August, issue
the call to mass action.

As soon as my teaching ended, my schedule became
set: I worked on my novel in the mornings, I ate lunch,
and I spent my afternoons and evenings working on the
national campaign—mimeographing material, writing letters, answering inquiries, telephoning, sending out copies
of the Stanford Statement, the press release, press clip-
pings, and Hartman's memo to every prominent individual and peace organization I could think of. I was, in
short, doing what I had dreamed of doing six years
before—and this time I was doing it publicly, I was enjoying it, and I was getting results.

The oppressiveness that had come to define New
York politics for me was gone in the spring and summer

of 1967. Nearly all the campus radicals were good three-man basketball players, and in the schoolyard a block from my house we'd play several afternoons a week, joking about jump shots and jail. On Sunday mornings we played softball. We went to meetings by foot and by car, not by subway; we met in backyards, in gardens; we demonstrated under the sun; we had picnics in Dave Harris' backyard; most of those who had committed themselves to resistance were also working with black activists in the East Palo Alto ghetto—working in the day-school program that members of that community had put in place of an Upward Bound program they'd thrown out. Things could, I felt at the time, be accomplished in the Bay Area of California that could never have been started amidst the political entrenchments of the Parade Committee, the geography of Manhattan Island.

We had come a long way from white armbands: Stanford now had more students pledged to draft resistance, over four hundred, than any college in the country —and Stanford only had about six thousand male students, graduate and undergraduate; through its former student body president, Dave Harris, it had become the organizing base for The Resistance, and for the October 16th turn-in of draft cards; and through its faculty, it was becoming the base for the first mass nationwide attempt at direct action by those beyond draft age.

There was something else, something more intangible—something I'd experienced before only when I'd been a boy and something I would experience again only after I'd arrived in Spéracèdes—a sense of community, of things held in common, of a world that was—if marginally, partially—shared. Betsey and I felt it slightly, and we liked it; those of draft age, we knew, probably felt it more than we did. A month or two after we'd arrived in Spéracèdes, Bill Wiser passed along a copy of *The Vil-*

lage Voice to me, and I found the following in it, from an interview with Emmett Schaeffer, a New York member of The Resistance. It articulated what I'd been feeling that summer about New York and California, and I clipped it out:

> The New York Resistance is almost wholly uncommunitarian. Very few draft resisters know each other, and even workers in the Resistance office conduct their extra-office lives in private. The California Resistance, on the other hand, is familial; many workers and organizers live together doing Movement work while one member holds an outside job to support the rest.
>
> There are a lot of advantages in that . . . People in California have each other's support. When you join the Resistance there you really join a community. And I think people there feel that they're building a continuing radical movement, not just an anti-war movement . . .
>
> . . . Resistance leaders talk a great deal about resistance as a process, a process of taking control of your life, of freeing yourself from the system which aims at channeling you toward its own approved goals, a process, in the end, of continuing radicalization. . . .

The initial response to our first mailings concerning the mass civil disobedience campaign was encouraging. We received endorsements from nationally known individuals, and from major peace organizations; we were assured privately that some of the nation's most prominent religious leaders (e.g., the Reverend Dr. King, Reinhold Niebuhr, Rabbi Herzberg) could "be delivered" if we could demonstrate that the numbers were there for mass civil disobedience; and we received good coverage in the periodicals which were most likely to reach our projected constituency.

At the same time, due in large part to the six-day Arab-Israeli War that June, there were signs that things in the middle-class middle of the peace movement were beginning to move in reverse. I received a letter, for example, from Noam Chomsky, who was working to organize some form of civil disobedience on the East Coast, in which he said that he had "received letters from a number of people saying, to my great surprise, that they now think perhaps the U.S. should be the policeman of the world (to save Israel, etc.). I think we will have to wait until things simmer down, and there is a return to rationality."

> The Stanford statement and the number of people who signed it, are very impressive. I doubt that we could even come close to those numbers here, among tenure faculty, at least, in all the Boston area universities put together.

My 10 percent–90 percent theory began to fall apart. In the jargon of the press, doves (on Vietnam) were becoming hawks (on Israel). Many who had, at first, been sympathetic to our proposals now began to question closing down the Pentagon, immobilizing induction centers. Might we not, as the argument went once more, "alienate" those moderates whose support we needed and had been (for so many years) trying to enlist?

Most of those who remained responsive to the idea of civil disobedience now began to shy away from actual confrontation and sought (again) for symbolic confrontation—for acts which had as much (or more) to do with establishing the *right* to protest the war as they did with protesting the war. I received letters from people urging that we put our major efforts into "The Call to Resist Illegitimate Authority"—a statement which had been drawn up earlier that summer and which gave technically "illegal" support to draft resisters.

Although I'd helped in the early stages of organizing

for the "Call," I remained unenthusiastic about it. I enlisted signers for it, but I kept urging people—in person, in
letters—to choose an action which did more than merely
provoke a "legal and moral confrontation" with the government; I urged them to risk more of themselves, to take
some action which did not simply support draft resistance
by a signature, but which, as Hartman had put it, in some
way was "analogous" to draft resistance.

In mid-August, Vietnam Summer officially separated
itself from us. "I *have* been trying to talk up, organize, etc.
around the civil disobedience issue you have started in
Palo Alto," Hartman wrote me, "and although most persons are interested, they seem not to give it high priority.
. . ." He referred me to Resist, the organization which
was working to get signatures for "The Call To Resist Illegitimate Authority," and to the National Mobilization
Committee (under Dave Dellinger), which was, by then,
talking about a "direct action component" in the October
16–21 Pentagon demonstration.

In Palo Alto, we called a meeting of all the local
peace groups and decided to organize for direct action
against a specific target on the West Coast, and to try, by
our example, to get others to organize similar actions in
other parts of the country. Our original target date of
late-August early-September was by now abandoned; we
agreed, instead, to organize around the week of October
16—the date chosen by The Resistance for the sending
back of draft cards. Activity—meetings, letters, phone
calls—continued, and, on a local level, the possibility for
substantial united action seemed good. We had a strong
group of committed activists, representing substantial
local constituencies—Stanford faculty, local clergy, high
school students, the Resistance, Joan Baez' Institute, Palo
Alto Concerned Citizens, East Palo Alto black activists,
the West Coast War Resisters League, the local Vietnam

Summer people—and we were soon in touch with other Bay Area groups who were also organizing for the week of October 16.

By this time, however, I was discouraged, depressed. Again, as before, I had been too optimistic, and my disappointment now was as intense as my hopes had been. I felt tired. The turn-in of draft cards would be nationwide —but it would be negligible, it would have little effect on the government's ability to carry on the war. It could not compare, in scale, to the nationwide campaigns I'd previously envisioned—either in reality, or in my imagination. The local work that was continuing—and increasing —was important, and I continued to be part of it, but without enthusiasm. I felt even more discouraged and disillusioned than I'd felt a year before, when I'd tried (and failed) to get the mass civil disobedience campaign going in New York.

The effect on the antiwar movement of the Arab-Israeli War, the focus of antiwar activity on "support" for draft resistance, the withdrawal of Vietnam Summer from the plan—everything seemed to confirm my feeling that, though the antiwar movement had grown, once again—at most—it had only grown in proportion to the growth of the war, and to the government's ability to absorb protest against the war. All things were as they had always been. *Plus ça change . . .*

By this time I had also finished my new novel and it had been accepted for publication. I felt drained, and until I began another novel I would, I knew, live with what was still my most terrible fear—that I had nothing left to say, that I would never write again.

Stanford offered me a position for the fall, but I said no, and at the end of August Betsey and I followed through on the plans we'd begun a year before and bought ship tickets, sailing date, September 29, 1967. I saw no reason for staying, nothing that I could do that would be crucial, nothing that might happen that I would want to be part of. And I was relieved to know that I'd be gone before the week of October 16—for the actual events, I feared, would have moved me, pulled on me, gotten me caught up in things all over again.

During the latter part of the summer I went to several meetings in San Francisco, held in the offices of *The Movement* (a SNCC-affiliated newspaper), at which we organized to try to shut down the Oakland Induction Center. "We have come together," the call we issued said, "not to engage in a gesture of discontent, not to register symbolic protest, not to influence those in power—but to exercise power." In San Francisco, things were different than they'd ever been in New York. "We know that one week of activity against the induction centers—even if we close them down across the country—will not stop the draft," our call stated. "We see this week as a way of involving young people who are facing conscription: black people, high school students, the unemployed and young working people."

In Palo Alto we began organizing in small groups of fifteen to twenty people; these groups would meet often between August and October 16, so that demonstrators would learn how to regroup quickly in the midst of an action, among people they knew, in order to decide on strategy, counterstrategy, tactics. That most people seemed to accept the fact that our action did not begin and end (win or lose) with the induction centers (or even with this particular war) seemed right to me, and I remember, during our last weeks in California, speaking with friends about the possibility of building a radical political movement which would be capable of enduring the daily and yearly ups and downs of events, of the government's actions, of the country's war and antiwar sentiment, and even of our own half-formed notions of where we were, why, and what had to be done about it.

I arrived in New York in early September and found that the New York antiwar organizations were in their usual state of frenzied factionalism. I met with people from Resist, the War Resisters League, the Parade Committee, the National Mobilization Committee, and told them about what we'd been doing in California. Although Spock and others were already enlisted on behalf of civil disobedience, nobody yet knew (less than a month before October 16) what the form of the civil disobedience would be—or where it would be.

After a year in Palo Alto, everything in New York seemed brutal, difficult—even the subways, which I'd loved passionately, tired me. The fact that, when meetings were over, people dispersed to invisible corners of the five boroughs, to apartment houses where they didn't speak to or know their neighbors; the fact that the simple matter of trying to meet with friends, or with people in antiwar groups, became, always, a major logistical problem; the fact that hair-splitting on texts and arguing over objectives seemed to be a more highly developed art form than it had been a year before; the fact that talk still seemed to be equivalent to action, that people seemed to feel they'd done something concrete against the war in Vietnam when they'd spent an hour or an evening in New York arguing with someone about it—all of this seemed absurd, hopeless, painful; all of it made me ache to get away.

At the beginning of the summer, Mitchell Goodman had gone East, and had printed a brochure ("TO THE CLERGY, THE MEN and WOMEN of the PROFESSIONS, THE TEACHERS: A CALL FOR CONSCIENTIOUS RESISTANCE TO THE WAR AND TO THE THREAT OF MILITARISM") in which the Stanford

Statement, along with quotes from Hartman and endorsements already secured from prominent individuals had been reprinted ("HOW IT BEGAN: THE STANFORD PLEDGE"). With this material he'd been working to organize what eventually became the Justice Department confrontation leading to the case of the United States vs. Spock, Coffin, Goodman, Ferber, and Raskin.

Mitch and I spoke often, and he tried to get me to stay. One letter from him, with an allusion to the old Black Sox scandals (". . . we need you . . . I've told many people here in the east how much you did out there . . . you can't start a thing like this, encourage people to civil disobedience—and then not be there. Say it isn't so.") touched me where I was weak, aroused some guilt, made me consider changing my plans, but only for a day or two. On September 29, we left America.

SEVEN: *Home*

We are reverting to the civilization of luggage,
and historians of the future will note how the middle classes accreted possessions without taking
root in the earth, and may find in this the secret of
their imaginative poverty.

—E. M. Forster. *Howard's End.*

I left America, retreated into a more private world
than any I'd been living in, and I found that even the
need to justify this retreat diminished with time, then
disappeared.

My desire (need) to persuade others of the validity of
my views—or even to attempt to explain to myself the
meaning of my actions, my choices, of my more obscure
and/or apocalyptic statements (without revolution, America is doomed)—this desire passed also. When I first arrived in Europe, I remember, I hungered for news of
America—I couldn't begin a day until I'd bought and
read the *International Herald Tribune*. This stopped also:
in Spéracèdes weeks would go by when I wouldn't see a
newspaper. From time to time, an article in a paper I did
see, a letter from a friend, a specific memory, an encoun-
ter with an American abroad, news of the war, of the
cities—these could arouse me, arouse my desire to return,

to do something—but only temporarily. The longer I stayed away from America, the easier—up to a point—it became to stay away. Major events—the assassinations of King and Kennedy; the Spock Trial; ghetto riots; student rebellions; the Democratic and Republican conventions in the summer of 1968; the New York City teachers strike —these only reinforced my desire to stay away.

One exception: during the week of October 16, 1967—just after we'd arrived in Europe—when news of the demonstrations at the Pentagon and the Oakland Induction Center reached London, I craved to go back. The size and scale of the actions stunned me—in Washington, demonstrators had actually penetrated the Pentagon, and in Oakland, the plans we'd made seemed to be working: demonstrators working in teams, the induction center shut down temporarily, the Oakland police (this was most astonishing) having to call to other cities for reinforcements. I got all the reports I could, I talked nonstop about what was happening with another Stanford teacher, a doctor from the medical school who was working at the National Health Institute in London, and who had been involved in organizing the Oakland Induction Center action—we talked of flying back to America. In Oakland, we told ourselves, something new was happening—something that might even be the beginning of actual revolutionary activity in which white and black radicals would be allies.

In the end, after releasing energy, frustration in a fight to storm the American Embassy in London, after securing bruises which I could carry proudly for several weeks (cherishing them as I'd cherished football injuries when I was younger)—I was glad I hadn't followed the impulse to go back. Nothing would have been served, the actions—again—were largely symbolic. The war continued, continued to escalate.

Something else, of course—something that seemed, at the time, too selfish, self-centered, to tolerate in myself. My vanity was hurt; I'd misjudged the course events would take, and now that events which I'd played a role in planning were at the center of the world's attention, I wanted some of the credit. It was difficult, for a few days, to resign myself to my fate: I would not be there to reap the kinds of public dividends that the letter to Kennedy had once promised, and which might now have been mine.

This was not the worst blow my vanity suffered that week. During the battle to break into the Embassy, Betsey and I had been in the front lines, pushing and shoving against the London police. Betsey, in fact, after having argued with me during the walk across London against my infatuation with techniques, as in Oakland, which were not nonviolent—had been the only one of thousands to break through the police lines. She did so three times, and then—caught in no-man's-land between the police and the Embassy—she'd called to thousands of us to follow her. At which point, each time, she was gingerly lifted up by a policeman and placed back in the crowd. At one point, sweating and groaning, I'd looked up to find myself staring into a beautiful red beard, trimmed beefeater fashion, like that of the guard at the Tower of London. The owner of the beard, a young London policeman, his arms linked with those of his co-workers to right and left, was groaning and sweating also. "With a beard like that," I muttered, "you should be on our side." As we continued to shove against one another, three to four thousand people behind me, five hundred to a thousand police behind him, mounted horses now beginning to help, without even seeming to notice me, with only the slightest glance my way, he replied at once, *"I've got taste."*

During the next eighteen months I was involved in only one other incident which was in any way political. In the fall of 1968—a year after we'd left America, and just after Betsey and I had returned from the camping trip which had taken us across 9,000 miles of Europe, from the arctic circle in Norway to the inner regions of Yugoslavia—I received a notice from my draft board stating that the FBI and the Attorney General had informed them that I had "surrendered" my draft card, and that they would, therefore "be forced to take action" against me—unless, of course, I now promised to carry the card with me and to obey all parts of the selective service law. Two weeks after the first notice, I was directed "to report" to my local board. What had seemed, only four months before—when I wrote the reflections with which this book begins—a "remote" possibility, was no longer remote.

Betsey and I had gone on the long trip that summer —away from Spéracèdes—for several reasons. In her third month, five weeks after we'd received the news that she was pregnant, she'd suffered a miscarriage, and we'd been more let down, more shaken by this than we'd expected to be. Also, I'd come to the point in this narrative where I'd begun chronicling my New York and California antiwar and civil rights activities, and having to do so had filled me with distaste for the entire project. I had absolutely no desire to write about meetings and marches, wars and ghettos—and, realizing that I didn't want to write, in a supposedly political book, about the years when I had, finally, become political, I had to doubt the book itself, my reasons for doing it, whether or not I should continue. My second novel had been published a few months before, and, for me, this meant that I should have been working on the third. Instead—again— politics (in the form of a book) was in the way.

The trip helped. When I returned to Spéracèdes in the fall, I was able to dig in at once on the final chapters of this book, and though everything I'd written on my thirtieth birthday, and everything I'd said in the final chapter of the original draft of this book should have made me react, when I heard from my draft board, in whatever "realistic" way would have most easily solved the immediate problem—I reacted, inevitably, in an opposite way. I refused to reply to my draft board, I refused to promise them anything, and I swore that I would not. My moral juices were as active as they'd ever been: I wrote long letters to friends and antiwar organizations telling them of my predicament, and explaining why I would not, of course, ask for my draft card back—even though I was thirty years old, even though I still had a 2A deferment (leave of absence from teaching), even though this meant that being declared delinquent I would be called for induction in the next month's pool, and, when I didn't report, would be faced with the usual penalties: five years in jail and/or $10,000 fine.

I would, I said, probably get to stay on in Spéracèdes indefinitely. For, I argued, if the government could, by threatening jail, get me to say: "Okay, I'll ask you to send me back my draft card"—then what had all my protests ever meant? Although the draft card was only a piece of paper sent out by people who had no "legitimate" authority to conscript men and send them to kill and be killed, that piece of paper was important: for it represented the government's actual ability to have killed all the people it had already killed in Vietnam. Although I admitted to those who suggested that I simply ask for the card back, that nothing would be served by my exile, that I myself had—since at least a year before—been of the opinion that draft card turn-ins were morally noble acts, but politically useless ones, I now stood firm.

Then too, though I was, by turns, enraged, obsessed, made giddy by what was happening—did the American government, or its bureaucracy, actually want to put me in jail?—the fact that I might have to go to jail or face not returning to America for many years didn't, during a Spéracèdes autumn, seem very real.

The day I'd received my first note from my draft board, I'd written to Resist, the major organization for aiding resisters, asking for advice on how to keep out of jail. By the time I received—exactly one month later—a notice from my local board declaring me "delinquent," I had not yet received a reply from Resist, or from any of the other antiwar organizations I'd written to. But I was far from America, I was over thirty years old, I was married, my writing was going well, I would be able to survive—what, I wondered, would have happened to an eighteen-year-old in my position who needed to rely on the efficiency and machinery of the American peace movement?

After not hearing from Resist, I'd also written to a friend of mine, Marty Cramer. He was a lawyer and I'd asked for his advice; I now received it. "My advice to you," he wrote, "is to swallow your PRIDE and to write the Draft Board that you were away when the letters came and could not answer them. Tell them to return your draft card. period." He pointed out some consequences of my action I hadn't thought of (e.g., the problems I might have getting my passport renewed if I stayed abroad to avoid prosecution, the problems I might have putting up with the laws of whatever other country I chose to live in), and said a few other things which part of me had already been whispering.

My brief research shows that the law requiring persons to carry a draft card is merely an extension of the law which requires you to register for the Draft at age

18. The penalty for not carrying is the same for not registering—up to 5 years and $10,000. Since you have already registered, and have carried the card for years— it seems foolish to make a moral issue out of this— especially since you now state that you don't particularly believe in handing in draft cards anymore . . . the only time that you should fight is when they actually decide to draft you . . . at this stage it seems ridiculous to thumb your nose at them and ask them to punish you for some silly little infraction. . . . Ask for the card back and say no more. . . . If you say it's a matter of conscience— I wont believe you because you have already admitted that draft card protests have no more meaning to you. Please write your draft board *now*.

He signed the letter—General Hershey.

An hour after his letter arrived I'd written to my draft board, telling them that they could return my card to me, and I'd delivered the letter to Georgette. I shook my head, then proceeded to visit each of my friends, telling them of what I'd done. The point, I said (still having to find some justification—moral, political, and metaphysical—for every action I took in this world), was not to give the shits who were killing us any more power than they already had. The point was not to be absolutely moral when dealing with amoral bureaucracies. The point was not to let one's life be destroyed in symbolic skirmishes. The point was to read carefully what I'd written on my thirtieth birthday . . . and there were, as always, many more points. I felt high, spun around, relieved—and then, strangely, almost drunkenly pleased with myself. Had I actually considered—for over a month—living in semipermanent exile? (Until I received a new draft card two months later—1A classification—the possibility that I hadn't written in time to counteract the delinquency notice would remain.) Once I'd asked for the card back, I had to wonder what had made me become so morally obstinate

—and once I wondered about this, I found myself smiling, dizzy with the knowledge that I had not, after all, changed so much in all the years since GM—since my first political campaign, and that first novel which had preceded (had prophesied) that campaign.

Our life continued in Spéracèdes—except that we now began to make plans for returning to America. There were no particular reasons for coming back—just the feeling that we wanted to (and that we wanted to return when we weren't forced to). If for nothing else, to see if —after Spéracèdes—we would be able to live in America —*si on pourrait supporter la vie là-bas.* I'd already accepted a teaching position in New York—at a new experimental college on Long Island (State University of New York, College at Old Westbury), where there would be, for the first two years, less than 250 students, where all administrators would also teach, where students would share fully in planning and decision making, where housing (on campus—in former servants' quarters) would be provided for us. It sounded ideal—if at some point we had to go back (because we wanted to), and if going back I would have to work somewhere (we would have to eat, we would have to live somewhere), I didn't think we would ever do much better than this: no hassle about finding a place to live, a college which—it seemed from the literature they were sending me—might have a greater sense of community, of "relevance" (every student would be required to spend at least one year away from the school working or studying—in ghettos, foreign countries, etc.) than most others. "Responsibility for one's own living and learning," the college catalog stated, "in college as in life, will be the operating principle."

Life in Spéracèdes was as it had been. The daily round of our life was the same, and—in good times and bad—we continued to share it with our friends. In the

winter of 1968–69, the bad times outnumbered the good
(Nancy Cusack died, some close friends went through bad
times, other families talked of leaving Spéracèdes). But the
essential quality of our lives remained good, whole. Betsey
and I spent more time than we ever had with our friends—
and with each other. We still woke early, I walked into
town for the day's bread, we ate breakfast together, I got
the mail, I went up to my room to work (to read, write,
stare at the sea), Betsey painted, we had long leisurely
lunches, took walks, brief trips to nearby villages, spent
evenings with friends, or at home, reading, talking.

Our refrigerator had now been borrowed by
Clément for his store, and, plugged in twenty-four-hours
a day, it became the village's frozen food department.
Bene finished building his house and we had a huge feast
to celebrate—in fact, Sundays had become ritual days for
feasts; every week we seemed to find one excuse or
another—and when we didn't have excuses, we had the
feasts anyway: all of us together (with children, our
group would number between thirty and forty), singing,
talking, drinking, eating *cous-cous* or *paella* or lamb
(which we'd roast—whole or half—over an open pit), playing *boules*, gathering in the *bistro* for coffee and more
drinks.

And, as noted, the first draft of this book finished—
and several other projects completed (a collection of stories, a screenplay)—my own desire to write seemed gone,
and I didn't mind. We considered changing our plans
from time to time—we told ourselves that our life in
Spéracèdes was good, that we were happy together there,
that—if we left and then returned—things would not be
the same, that we would not find a comparable life anywhere in America, that there was still time to turn down
the job and just stay on—but in the end we always came
to the conclusion that we wanted to go back, that we

would stick to our plans. We would see friends and family, we would put away some money again—if things became intolerable for us—we could always pick up and leave, return to Spéracèdes. (Clément and Fernande told us that they would not rent our house in September until we told them—100 percent—that we were not coming back.)

At the end of March, after parties, tears, good-byes, we set sail from Cannes (Betsey's paintings rolled up and hidden in our trunks to hide them from French customs —who didn't even bother to look; all paintings which leave France must be passed on by the Beaux-Arts)—and ten days later, we arrived in America, where the U. S. customs agent opened every one of our packages, every piece of luggage, made us wash dried mud from our boots, tapped on the sides of our trunks in search of false compartments, went through the titles of our books. We drove across the city and when I stopped for gas, a young black guy in a baseball cap, eyes at half-mast, held the pump hose and asked me about the foreign license plate on my car—my first conversation in America. I told him we'd just returned from over a year and a half in France.

He shook his head. "Oh man," he asked. "*Why'd* you come back?" His eyes opened. "Man," he said, "it's worse here than Vietnam. . . . Soon as I get through school, I'm gettin' out."

That morning, after not having slept all night, Betsey and I had come on deck just before six—at the moment that our ship passed under the Verrazano Bridge. The ship turned, headed toward Manhattan Island. The skyline seemed changed—squarer, less varied. The city looked vast, huge—and something I hadn't expected—strong. It didn't, however, look good; it did not, as I'd expected it would, feel good to be home. As the ship made its way up the Hudson—as we passed downtown, the

Lower West Side—I spoke for the first time: "Bring this
down—?" I said. "Not a chance." Stop it—maybe . . . par-
alyze it from time to time—but destroy it, overthrow it
(whatever that might mean)—never. Okay, I said to myself
—even before we'd left the pier (listening to the dock
workers, looking at the muddy, filthy water, watching the
gulls, watching a longshoreman slip a huge payoff to a
customs inspector, having to go through every item I'd
brought back with me)—okay, this is what you came back
for—if only for five minutes: you made the right decision,
you had to return, you'll write the new novel.

There were, predictably, too many impressions at
first. Things were big, dirty, noisy, overwhelming. Cars
were enormous. People's faces were gray, and sad. The
bright-colored clothes, draped on tired bodies, unsmiling
faces (sometimes the complexions seemed almost univer-
sally jaundiced), made Americans look like dolls with
glaring doll's clothing. Especially so with old people—
women with painted hair and lips; men in absurdly
bright colors.

Life seemed hard, people seemed unhappy, food was
dreadful—I spent much of my first week reading the lists
of chemicals on all the packaged food I ate—everybody
seemed to work hard, even when they were not working,
all of life—work, friendships, family—seemed fragmented,
compartmentalized, the opposite of what it had been in
Spéracèdes. In my memory, the German and Swiss people we'd met on our trip—my sense of their lives—made
them now seem like relaxed Mediterraneans. Conversations tired me more than I believed possible—everything
one said, even in passing, among friends, seemed to have
some object. Conversation was not merely conversation;
it seemed to need, always, to have some issue, some
profit, some gain. Everything—even in the newest, most
modern parts of the city and Long Island seemed to be

temporary, in a state of disrepair. And yet, as I sensed such things during my first few days back, despite the fact that everything seemed to be in some stage of deterioration, the country seemed unbelievably strong. For so much waste to exist in the midst of so much affluence (my only theory during my first week), the basic productive power of the economy (and the empire) had to be enormous.

The school I was to teach at was a disappointment. The fault, again, as at GM, probably lay in me, in my expectations. Had I actually believed that a radically experimental college could be sponsored by the state of New York? Had I really hoped that—amidst the expressways and shopping centers and suburban towns of Long Island —one could have an island of relevance, a genuine community? With only eighty-three students, I discovered, the college was already a full-scale bureaucracy. There were, by count, more full-time administrators (fourteen) than faculty (eleven), and the total support staff— secretaries seemed to be everywhere—numbered over sixty. I received three or four memos a day—reports, studies, notices for committee meetings, evaluations of reports; in the president's office there were shelves lined with over seventy different handouts, mostly reprints of his own speeches about the new experimental college of the State University of New York.

The total number of full-time faculty and administrators (I couldn't keep track of the part-time teachers, consultants, and staff) was twenty-five, and there seemed to be almost that many political factions. I was staggered— depressed—most by the sheer amount of mistrust and double-dealing that one year had bred—business on campus seemed to be conducted as much by rumor, gossip, and private denunciation as by anything else. Faculty members despised one another, and said so. Several of the faculty who supported the president against the students, at the same time drafted a letter to Albany, asking for the president's resignation, a letter they were ready to use should the president have lost a major battle with the students.

The housing which had been promised to us had disappeared (as we were about to arrive, the school discovered that it had promised and given out more campus housing—less than ten spots—than it had), but at the last minute temporary quarters were found for us. Two weeks before we'd sailed I'd had what was probably my best indication of what was to come when I'd received a telegram asking if I could report the following September, instead of in April—this after I'd sent letters, over the course of a year, asking, in each one, exactly when I would be needed on campus and what my duties would be when I got there. When I arrived, administrators began asking me what *I* would like to do. A seminar they had hoped I would, upon my arrival, "save," had dissolved sometime during the ten days it took for me to cross the ocean—why then, they suggested, didn't I "take my time" and use the months of April and May "to get to know people"? For this, I gasped, I would be paid over $1000 a month. As for the promise of partnership for students— though the mandate of the school, made official in the State University's 1966 *Master Plan,* stated that the college "would admit students to full partnership in the academic world," this was taken by the administration to mean that students would be "consulted" on all major decisions; administrators would, still, make the final decisions themselves. They did. Thus, though a joint student-faculty committee to select new faculty had, in the absence of departments, submitted a list of ten new faculty recommendations to the president—the president had vetoed two of the ten choices, and had made an offer to another faculty prospect who had been rejected by the faculty selection committee. Not a bad percentage, of course, but—given the fact that nobody could recall the last time a president of a major college or university had vetoed even a single faculty recommendation, and given the particular mandate of the college at Old Westbury—this became one fact among many that the students would decide they couldn't live with. And so —seven weeks after I arrived—confrontation, occupation of buildings, a sit-in, student demands—and (as someone pointed out to me I'd predicted in what I'd written on my thirtieth birthday) I found myself on the side of the students, in the buildings, drafting—on the first day— a statement of no confidence in the president and of support for the students which I got the majority of the faculty to sign.

But such things—political, personal, predictable— were not what impressed me most about the school. It was—despite its miniature size—a college like other colleges; it was neither "relevant" nor "experimental" (by the following fall the college, which had been given a virtual carte blanche for innovation and experimentation, had settled down to a vague program, one which virtually excluded "field work" for all but those students specializing in Urban Studies, and one which included three programs: a Disciplines College (courses in modern literature and philosophy), a standard model Urban Studies College, and—for everybody else—a General Program that had already been tried and tested for four years at San José State College.) The college was, however, still different in one crucial way—in its claim to be different. This was a college which had been asked by the Chancellor of the State University of New York "to review all the conventional ingredients . . . and break whatever barriers may be in the way." It was a college which tried endlessly to explain away the phrase "full partnership"—but which would not give it up.

By the fall of 1969 the start of its second pilot year, the president—a former Associate Director of the Peace Corps, an adviser to President Kennedy on civil rights, a lawyer with a special interest in civil liberties—had resigned to become president of Bryn Mawr. His own understanding of educational innovation, experiment, and civil liberties was evidenced for me several weeks after I arrived, when the student literary magazine was seized from the mailing room and not permitted to go out to students, because, as the president explained in a letter to the editor, it would probably be judged to be "obscene." While "as a lawyer," he said, he might defend the magazine's "right to publish" what it chose, he was still an "officer of the University"; his reason for seizing the magazine then, was because it was his judgment that its contents—specifically, a cartoon by R. Crumb, reprinted from *Head-Comix*—might "offend the moral views of the majority of the people of New York State who support this college." (When he first saw the magazine, the president had sent a messenger to the office of admissions to find out if R. Crumb was going to be an Old Westbury student the following fall.)

All of this, then, was not surprising, and, after a month or two I seemed to get used to it. What continued to amaze me, what still amazes me after a half year back was something else: the funds that kept being poured into the college for buildings, supplies, consultants, salaries, secretaries, programs, printing, cars. Where, I kept asking, was all that money coming from?

I felt, I said during the first few weeks, like Ralph Ellison's Invisible Man—i.e., that I was, quite literally, plugged into the nation's power supply: I received housing, an office, a telephone; my postage was paid for, my writing supplies were provided (there was a carton of supplies on my desk when I arrived—appointment calendar, marble stand with pen, paper, pads, stapler, stapler

remover, tape, boxes of throw-a-way manifold carbon
paper sets—in which a sheet of carbon paper was used
only one time ("Your time is worth more to your employer typing than salvaging carbon paper.")—this after
years of making four and five carbon copies of novels and
stories on my portable typewriter, trying to figure out
whether to use each carbon nine, ten, or eleven times);
and—most amazing of all—there were new state cars with
official state seals on their sides, available for my use.
(For its eighty-three students and two dozen faculty and
administrators, there were five state cars; when the school
grew to 222 students—and to a staff of over 100—in the fall
of 1969, five additional cars were delivered.) How, I kept
wondering, could this be? How could the system support
so many planners, so much nonproductive labor and material?

Where, I kept asking, was all the money coming
from? The school's operating budget was slightly over
one million dollars for the first year, slightly under two
million for the second year (the cars came out of a separate
budget in Albany, and not out of the school's budget). In
a speech given shortly before his resignation, the college
president revealed that the "promise of 'full partnership'"
was "taken from an early memorandum on the college by
[the Vice Chancellor], which was written in the aftermath
of the explosion at Berkeley, at a time when the University
was anxious to get ahead of the student revolution." The ad-
vance construction budget for building a school whose ori-
gin, whose reason for existence, lay in such notions—for
building a school that would have a maximum of five
thousand students when completed, was—I still can't believe it (and the figure will doubtless be higher by the
time construction is finished)—one hundred million dollars.

As at GM, I began generalizing (if such waste and
wealth were running wild at one *college* . . .), and devis-

ing antic, silent schemes. When the school had its year-end review session I would have only one question: why was a state car available for a professor but not for a welfare recipient?

The school, I said (to myself at first—later to others) was an obscenity and should be closed. We had to take away from the state its ability—its right—to claim that it had an experimental college. Take the money, give it to the Black Panthers, and let them fund us as a free university. Take the money—and just give it away. Why, I asked, was the editor of Time-Life Books, and not one of the school electricians or gardeners, the head of the College Council? And why were students walking across gardens and lawns which they didn't tend? How could the school consider itself real—set off on the six-hundred-acre estate and arboretum of William Robertson Coe (owner of several other estates, including Buffalo Bill's 200,000-acre ranch in Cody, Wyoming)—when it had no village store? no *bistro*?

Betsey and I tried, in our own lives, to maintain as much of what had been good in Spéracèdes as possible—and six months later, we still try: we have no television, no telephone, we buy no newspapers. Though we've given up on getting fresh vegetables (those that are called fresh seem to spoil overnight if left out of the refrigerator), or eggs that have taste (the mass-produced eggs in France, Jacques had said, were made by "concentration-camp chickens")—we still eat long leisurely lunches, which we prepare together, we still take walks after lunch. But life in Spéracèdes, as I'd written over a year before, had "unfitted me for a return to American civilization"—especially to life on Long Island, where everything seems to move on superhighways, where all essential relations (shopping, getting the mail, working) seem impersonal, where everything is arranged and communicated by telephone. And most of all, where the possibility of friendship—built and sustained on a daily basis in a world where the essential parts of day-to-day life are actually and physically shared—is almost nonexistent.

In fact, the only time during my first six months back in America when I felt that I'd been lifted from the severe depression which had immediately become my life was during the student sit-in at the end of the school year. After a few days of living in buildings with students and faculty, I realized that I felt good—and I knew why, made as many analogies as I could. For the week that we occupied buildings—even though the world we lived in was artificial, temporary—we were returned to essential functions: getting food, preparing meals, eating, sleeping, talking. For the first—the only—time, when I would meet somebody, instead of talking about a subject, we would talk about one another—I'd just seen X walking out of the dormitory; Betsey was making a batch of cookies to bring for lunch; Y was looking tired; How did you sleep last night? What was the weather going to be like? So-and-so seemed to be in good form today.

That we shared political enemies, political theories, and political objectives—all right; more important that—if briefly, artificially—I was in a situation among people I was coming to know and like and admire, I was in a situation where, when nobody was talking, I didn't mind the silence.

"At least," I would say to people during my first few months back, "it's good to know that the war in Vietnam is over." My cynicism trying vainly to mask my frustration, to excuse, in some arch way, the fact that—back in America—I felt (feel) no desire to become involved again in protest against the war, in politics. Not reading papers or watching TV or listening to the news on the radio, it was impossible, walking the streets of the nation, to know there was a war going on in which at least a half million

American soldiers were fighting. Despite my perverse refusal to listen to news or to discuss politics, attitudes and
opinions trickled in: the entire country, it now seemed,
agreed that the war in Vietnam should be ended—how
then, could it be that the actual numbers of men in Vietnam, the actual amount of bombing and destruction, the
weekly numbers of dead and wounded were greater than
they had been two years before, when only a minority of
Americans were against the war?

The peace movement, people would tell me, had accomplished a lot in changing the attitudes of Americans
toward the war. What was I to do with such a statement?
If most Americans were against the war—if the American
people had voted in two presidential elections for disen-
gagement from the war—and if the war was larger than it
had ever been, the murder and death and destruction
greater than they'd ever been, what conclusions did this
lead to—about the relation of democratic processes to
processes of government, about all the wealth and waste
which, home again, assaulted my imagination?

(An item noted just before I left Spéracèdes: one air-
line company giving a subcontract to another company to
develop—not produce—new in-flight ideas for mixes of
movies and music and tapes; cost—over ten million
dollars—though I didn't know what to do with such a
fact, like the existence of new state cars for faculty members, it seemed to tell me everything I needed to know.
Cf., also, my experience working with open housing committees in New York, where I would go in to see about
renting an apartment after a nonwhite person had gone
in. If, in 1964 and 1965 (before that phenomenon mis-
named backlash), in the most liberal city in the most liberal state in America, a city and state which had the
strongest antidiscrimination laws in the nation, doctors
and lawyers and businessmen who could afford $600-a-

month apartments still needed such a committee, were still being refused housing because of race—then this too was all I needed to know in order to imagine what things were like elsewhere, for people without such education, money, position.)

Nothing mattered except what happened: the only yardstick for measuring political protest, I said before we left Spéracèdes, was to ask if it affected the Stock Market or the Gross National Product. The rest, as Jacques would put it, "c'est de la littérature." But I drew no conclusions from my observations, impressions: I felt, I suppose, what I'd felt before—working in a single community, protesting a particular issue, closing down a particular school, teaching a particular human being—this was work which had nothing to do with those large things which trapped, wounded, and murdered people, and which preserved the continuity of such processes—but, as always, one did the best one could where one could.

Politics, however, in any overt form (except for the minor business at the college), did not now concern me. Having had, for a while, a place to live which we loved, where we lived—and how—seemed suddenly central, all important. Outwardly, back in America, things could not have been better. My life, in September of 1969, had the elements which might have been the matter for the happy ending—the epilogue—of a nineteenth-century novel: Betsey was pregnant again, and, in her seventh month, doing beautifully; I was succeeding beyond any previous hopes with my writing, and (something I'd never let myself hope would be possible) earning enough from it for us to live on; Betsey was painting and we were still spending most days—all day—together; my brother and mother and father were all well and I was relaxed in their company, I enjoyed being with them (for the first time, my father and I could sit in a room together, not speak-

ing, and I could—as I'd done with friends in Spéracèdes
—simply enjoy his presence).

Still, this wasn't enough—still we found (find) ourselves longing for Spéracèdes, find ourselves unable to
accept—as real or necessary—life on Long Island, in
America. A luxury, of course—symptomatic of the wealth
and waste of the land—to even be able to debate the relative merits of Spéracèdes and the United States, to have
the choice of one or the other, to even be able to write a
narrative such as this, one in which I can reflect on such
decisions, on ten years of my life. (Cf., students at Old
Westbury considering what *kind* of college they would
like to have. Consider—I had not, until I was back here—
what the reaction of a North Vietnamese might be to an
ad in *The New York Review of Books* for the *Vietnam
Curriculum,* to the fact that, while we wage war against
them, we are also able—we are free, in the most literal
sense—to debate the rightness and wrongness of what we
are doing, to absorb the war into our schools for study
and debate. Or, to put it another way, as one young Eng-
lishman put it to me, during my second week in Europe:
"Funny, ain't it—that all you Yanks get to come here for
your vacations, but I never get to spend my summers in
your country—")

The problem, then, luxurious as it is: having lived in
Spéracèdes and having tasted, over the course of sixteen
months, the kind of daily life there that I did, I find that I
cannot (do not want to) live here. And it will not, I
suspect—sense—be substantially different anywhere in
America—in California or the Northwest or on a farm in
upstate New York or a commune in New Mexico; one
goes (I would go) to these places to escape America, and
my life would be defined by this escape, by opposition. I
would still be living in America, and by now, this obviously has a particular meaning for me. As with the col-

lege at Old Westbury, I would say, so with other things: since Old Westbury is in America—part of America—why should (how could) it be better than, different from, America?

Yet—the part I have no reasons for, cannot analyze —I know I can't live any place but in America. A question—it seems at first—of roots, of history, of my subject (for fiction). But more than this: at the least, I know that, for me, living even semipermanently anywhere outside of America—even in Spéracèdes—seems, in prospect, unreal. Something like the situation—the predicament—of a black man in America; or, minimally, in my own life, analogous to the form that predicament took in the life of one black man. "The most crucial time in my own development," James Baldwin writes in his "Autobiographical Notes" for *Notes of a Native Son,* "came when I was forced to recognize that I was a kind of bastard of the West; when I followed the line of my past I did not find myself in Europe but in Africa. And this meant that in some subtle way, in a really profound way, I brought to Shakespeare, Bach, Rembrandt, to the stones of Paris, to the cathedral at Chartres, and to the Empire State Building, a special attitude. These were not really my creations, they did not contain my history; I might search in them in vain forever for any reflection of myself. I was an interloper; this was not my heritage. At the same time I had no other heritage which I could possibly hope to use —I had certainly been unfitted for the jungle or the tribe."

The problem—for Baldwin, too—has something luxurious about it; the terms of reference, the feelings are distinctly a writer's. They do not, at least at first, seem to deal with the everyday problems of masses of people who live in America's cities, trapped (at least at first) by things physical: color, ignorance, poverty.

Back in America, everything good—my writing, my
life with my wife, the times spent with friends—seems a
refuge from everything bad, from everything else. So,
while living and working here, Betsey and I talk endlessly to one another about our situation, about what
we'll do next—though lately it seems, we do this less.
Having found, temporarily, a place that was home for us,
a place in which we had a better life, day by day, than
we thought possible, we now find that we do not want to
settle for less; and we know that we are, at the moment,
lucky enough not to have to settle for less. Give things
time, we say—a year, a year and a half—and if life here is
still intolerable, if our friends are still there, we'll return
to Spéracèdes. Long-range plans and decisions stay unre-
solved, our life remains transient (we systematically shed
possessions)—and that's all right, too. The readiness, as always, is all.

I began this book, I thought, in order to trace my
own political activities—their origins, and where they
might lead; yet I end without having really done either—
I end without any conclusions, political or otherwise,
with—at the most—merely the attempt (doubtless an attempt which is politically counterrevolutionary) to discover, in terms more personal than political, who I am
and where I've been. I.e., in the fall of 1969 it seems
enough to be finishing the narrative of some of the things
which, in my own life, I thought had their beginnings at
General Motors in the summer of 1960—not in order to
persuade or convince or prove, but simply because it is
what I have been writing.

Spéracèdes, France—Old Westbury, New York
March, 1968—September, 1969

JAY NEUGEBOREN was born in Brooklyn, New York, in 1938. He is the author of two novels, *Big Man* and *Listen Ruben Fontanez,* and a book of short stories, *Corky's Brother.* His work has also appeared in *Best American Short Stories* (1965), *Prize Stories: O. Henry Awards* (1968), and in such magazines as *Commonweal, Commentary, Esquire,* and *New American Review* (No. 5). Mr. Neugeboren is married to the painter Betsey Neugeboren and has one child.